D1547382

~~asshole~~
attorney

~~asshole~~ attorney

MUSINGS, MEMORIES,
AND MISSTEPS
IN A FORTY-YEAR CAREER

Douglas J. Wood

For permission requests, contact the publisher at the website below.

Plum Bay Publishing, LLC
www.clairemckinneypr.com/plumbay

Library of Congress Control Number: 2018933568
ISBN: 978-0-9988617-2-2
Printed in the United States of America

Cover design by Lauren Harvey
Interior layout by Barbara Aronica-Buck
Edited by Jeremy N. Townsend and Kate Petrella

To my wife, Carol Ann, for putting up with me
and my stories for more than 50 years

contents

belvedere

the rest of the story

preface
Southern Inspiration

When I was a much younger lawyer, I handled a complicated breach of contract case where the two sides were more emotional than sensible about what they wanted. It was the classic example of clients losing sight of reality and more intent on hurting one another than amicably settling a difference. For greedy lawyers with wealthy clients, such cases are Nirvana.

The attorney on the other side was from Charleston, South Carolina. He was a stereotypical southern gentleman with a drawl that could melt solid rock. While our respective clients were about as unpleasant as they could be, he was always easygoing, honest, and forthcoming with his perspective. He knew as well as I did that we were both dealing with out-of-control clients.

After months of negotiations, we finally settled the case.

On the final telephone conversation I had with him, I commented, "You know, this is probably one of those cases where neither of our clients will be happy with us. Mine will undoubtedly complain she paid too much and your client will bitch that he got too little. So I imagine they'll blame it on the lawyers."

He responded in a deep, lilting southern drawl, "Doug, I been practicin' law for fifty years. And I learned a long time ago, there ain't no such word as 'attorney' or 'lawyer.' It's 'asshole attorney' or 'fuckin' lawyer.'"

It's with his blinding glimpse of reality that I was inspired to write this book, a collection of memories, experiences, and writings from my personal life and professional career. It's a book about asshole attorneys and fuckin' lawyers, and trust me: I've known plenty, including, on occasion, me.

Some of the folks who were there when the stories I tell happened will undoubtedly say, "Hey, why didn't you talk about [fill in name/event]." Or they might say, "I don't remember it that way." And some may even observe, "You should have never written about [fill in name/event]."

There will be some familiar with the stories who will laugh. Others will be angry with me.

There's a lot I didn't write about. I omitted names and stories about people for whom I have little, if any, respect. Usually they're people who also have little, if any, respect for me. To them, I really am an asshole attorney. To me, they're probably just plain assholes.

In some instances, I omitted events because they might embarrass or be hurtful to innocent people—even when some who were there might not think those who were spared the pointed pen are innocent. In omitting certain things, I also had to be sensitive about privileged or confidential information. So all the stories that relate to what I or others said are either public information or did not relate to any actual advice I may have given. I imagine some may disagree with that conclusion, but that's my story and I'm sticking to it.

For those who don't remember something the way I describe it, I concede that a few things might be a bit "edited."

In some instances, I admit I used creative license to keep the story interesting. In a few instances, I confess to exaggerating or enhancing some moments. But never did I veer from the truth of what happened.

The stories are as I remember them. Some who were there may remember them differently. That's human nature. I also have no doubt that some who were not there might have comments about what happened as well. I'll let that pass because I know they can't help themselves. Sort of like all the people who claimed they went to the Woodstock Festival in 1969 but never did. I admit I wasn't there.

Finally, to those who are unhappy about something I wrote, I offer no apology. Feel free to write about me. I have a thick skin.

I've written a leading treatise on advertising law, three novels in the historical fiction genre, and a book on advice I've given to my three children. I'm in the process of writing my fourth novel, another historical fiction thriller. All of them have done well and offend no one (at least no one has complained to me that they do).

So why would I write this book when I know it will not be embraced by some readers?

Good question.

I don't have a good answer. Perhaps it's my ego gone wild, buying the notion that others may actually find what I've done or said of interest. Or maybe it's my desire to relate the many wonderful and not so wonderful things that happened in my life and career in hopes that it will amuse or inspire a reader. It may be in response to the encouragement by the many people who have heard the stories and have told me that I should write the book. Or perhaps I want to leave a legacy for my grandchildren to read so they know a little about their grandfather, good and bad. Or it may just be part of the obsession many writers have that pushes them to write as a cathartic exercise that feeds their souls. It may be all of that or it may be something else I've missed. It really doesn't matter.

Someday, I'll guess I'll have to go into therapy and find the answer.

Until then, to my critics who pan my efforts, I say this: You try it. Put your money where your mouth is. You write a book about your life and the lessons you've learned. It isn't as easy as it sounds.

In the meantime, enjoy the stories.

family

chapter 1
My Early Hopes Shattered

I'm an army brat. What that means is that growing up for me meant moving from army base to army base every three years. By the time I was ten, I'd lived in Virginia, Pennsylvania, New Jersey, Hawaii, and Japan. With all the moves, we lived in eight different houses.

My dad retired when I was in fifth grade. At the time he retired, he was stationed in Schofield Barracks, Hawaii, and we lived about three blocks from one of the most beautiful beaches in the world. I played and swam there every day. In September 1960, we moved to Rutherford, New Jersey. Rutherford is about two hours from the Jersey shore and next to the Meadowlands, a misnomer at the time since it was actually a dumping ground and future Superfund site due to chemical contamination. The green water in the Passaic River was no comparison to the gin clear waters of Oahu. And I can't begin to describe how the Passaic smelled.

To my new classmates, I was an oddity. Most of them had no idea where Hawaii was, let alone how there could be this white kid who had a better tan than anyone in school, and who also wore pretty weird shirts. Back in the '60s, guys like me were way ahead of Tommy Bahama. And I didn't even wear shoes when I went to school in Hawaii's paradise. Barefoot was the rule. Now I had to wear long pants, plain shirts, socks, and shoes.

I was not happy.

If that weren't bad enough, I had never seen snow or at least never remembered seeing any of the stuff. So on the first day it snowed, I got excited, bundled up, and rushed outside to experience what everyone was telling me was terrific fun. I looked like Kenny from the series *South Park*. It took me less than a minute to realize I hated—and I mean *really* hated—snow and everything it represented.

That's when I was told the cold truth, no pun intended. I said to my mom, "Mom, we can't live here any more. We have to go back to Hawaii."

She responded, "Honey, that's not a decision for you to make. We live here now. Get over it." Or something like that.

I was crushed and resolved to dedicate my life to getting out and going back to paradise. I noticed that my neighbor was a lawyer, although I had no idea what that meant. None of my friends had parents who were lawyers. But our neighbor always seemed to be dapper and happy, carried a big, important-looking briefcase, and always said hello. So from what I observed, becoming a lawyer seemed as good a career as any to fund my escape from New Jersey. And when you're eleven years old, such impressions hold.

chapter 2
My Birth Family

My mom and dad—Rhoda and Gilbert Wood—were from that tough, World War II generation that saw working hard and being loyal as the two most important things one can do. But they were a lot of bark and very little bite. In fact, my dad, even though he was a hardened officer and Korean War veteran, never raised his hand to me and I cannot even remember him yelling at me. Discipline was left to my mom, and she wasn't very good at it. If my brother or I did something wrong, we were told to go outside and find a switch from a bush. When we brought it back, she'd whip us on our thighs. Trust me, the psychological terror of finding the switch was a lot worse than the swatting. I suppose if a parent did that today they'd be arrested for child abuse, but those were different times.

Both of my parents went out of their way to help me and give me advice. It was different for Gil, my older brother. He was the first-born son of a genuine war hero and a nurse who tended to the wounded in Pearl Harbor after the Japanese attack. So most of the pressure of following in my dad's footsteps fell on him. That was a lot of pressure that I was spared. Looking back, I only admire Gil more for what he experienced.

My sister, Martha, was always, as some daughters are, my dad's princess. Their relationship could not have been closer.

As the third and final child, seven years younger than my

brother and five years younger than my sister, I of course wondered if I was an afterthought, one of those "mistakes" parents make in the heat of an amorous moment. At least that's what my brother and sister loved to tell me over the objections of my mom. I used to fantasize that I was actually a prince left on the family stoop in a basket, one day reclaiming my kingdom. Right.

As is true with so many "thirds," I got away with murder. Other than the very rare occasion I was disciplined by Mom, I was barely noticed. And that drove my brother and sister mad. I can still hear their complaints: "How come Doug gets to do [fill in the blank]?" My ability to get away with mischief was the only source of revenge I had for all the innocent sibling harassment I got from them as the third child. And I loved getting away with it.

Growing up, I worshipped my brother, although I never let him know. He was the coolest guy I knew. Smart, handsome, great haircut, and sharp clothes. Pretty girlfriends. But he barely noticed me. We shared a room. He took glee in trying to scare me in the middle of the night. I always slept on my side of the room with my eyes toward him.

My sister was terrific, but I had no use for her as a kid. She was a girl. And she got a lot more attention from my dad and was never disciplined by Mom. She was just too perfect for me.

Today, my relationship with both is fantastic. My brother and I talk every week even though he lives in Romania. My sister and I speak less often, but it's always a great conversation.

chapter 3
The Crips and Bloods

In sixth grade, I joined a gang. It was called the RCH, for Rutherford Club House. We were also known as the "Boys." While not quite the Crips or Bloods, it was a real brotherhood and mutual protection pact. If you messed with any one of us, you messed with all of us. Kind of a neighborhood NATO. And while we rarely instigated anything, we had respect even from the "Hoods," the guys in school who were selling car parts before they had licenses to drive.

Founded by John "Frat" Frattarola, aka "The King," the RCH had a clubhouse in Frat's backyard. The gang included some official members: Frat, Deve, Arnie, Mers, Fred, Stein, Mute, Reit, Kell, John, Harv, Pop, Bruce, Burd, Beck, and me, and some unofficial members: Bennie, Rob, and Jarvis. I don't remember why the three unofficial members were never voted in, but they were a part of the RCH all the same. The other members had been close friends since kindergarten.

While three of our brothers—Mute, Bennie, and Burd—have passed away, and one (Jarvis) can't be found, the rest of us keep in touch. A small contingency comprised of Frat, Deve, Arnie, Stein, Harv, Pop, Fred, Mers, and Rob get together two or three times a year. Over the years, the Boys have taken three amazing private tours.

When we turned fifty-five, seven of us went on the "55 and Still Alive Booze, Blues, and Barbeque Tour" through Tennessee, Mississippi, and Arkansas, visiting the historical sites where the blues and rock 'n' roll were born, including Graceland, Stax Records, Sun Records, the Grand Ole Opry, Clarksdale, and more. Our bus driver, Jimmy, was an Elvis impersonator, and our bodyguard, "K," was from Egypt, packing some serious protection. Let's just say we went into some pretty seedy neighborhoods and K turned out to be a much-appreciated companion.

When we turned sixty, five of us went on the "60 and Still Nifty Orlando to Key West Margarita Tour." We took that trip in the campaign bus used by Barack Obama in his 2012 presidential campaign.

And when we turned sixty-five, six of us went on the "65 and Ready to Thrive Scotch, Shots, and Serenity Tour" through the Highlands of Scotland.

All these trips were just the Boys, no wives. And while it drove some wives up a tree that we went on such extravagant holidays without them, the wives of the Boys who went on the trips grudgingly put up with it. Other wives didn't, and the stay-at-homes missed out on memories that we still cherish to this day.

There were some magic moments on the tours.

When we finished our visit at Graceland, Arnie walked down from Elvis's grave and jokingly announced in his baritone voice, "Hey, I don't see what the big deal is. He's just another dead drug addict." Needless to say, the devoted fans there to pay homage to the King of rock 'n' roll didn't appreciate Arnie's joke. We had to get out of Graceland fast.

On the same trip, we visited Reds, a very famous blues

club in Clarksdale, Mississippi. I was the first to enter the club, at about 2:00 a.m. It was a scene out of *Animal House*. I was the only white guy in the room. Everyone, including the band, stopped and stared. So I walked up to the bar and asked, "What beer do you have?" The bartender answered, "Budweiser." I responded, "Great. I'll have a Bud. Mind if my friends come in?" He stared at me and said, "Sure. As long as they like Budweiser."

As if on cue, our Elvis impersonator walked in with the Boys in tow. K stayed with the bus. The place went wild. We were greeted as if we were long-lost friends. The band, led by blues greats T-Model Ford, Robert Balfour, Big T Williams and his sons, Mississippi Joe and Mississippi June Bug, rocked until dawn. And when Jimmy got on stage and did a set of Elvis tunes with them, it was something out of this world. In the end, we were all given new names: Mississippi Grease Plate Beck, Bigass Burd, Juke Joint Lawner, Short (Harv), Mojo Marcus (Stein), Blackcat Bone (Deve), Sticky Fingers Frat, and Cotton Seed Wood.

On our Orlando to Key West Tour we stayed at the Everglades Rod & Gun Club, where several U.S. presidents, Ernest Hemingway, and Mick Jagger once stayed. When they closed the bar, we reopened it, poured ourselves drinks, and evened up with the owners the next day. That was fine.

While in Scotland, we went to seven distilleries, three golf courses, castles, and medieval sites. A highlight was our visit to the Macallan distillery, where we drank eighteen-year-old scotch straight from a cask they rolled out of the barn. Deve gathered some in his hands and splashed it on like cologne. He loved it. Not sure if the rest of us did. We also saw the home on Trump's golf course that Trump surrounded with tall pines in order to block the owner's view when he refused to sell Trump the property. No wonder they hate Trump in Scotland.

To this day, over fifty years since I met the Boys, most of us are still together. Having friends for that long is unusual. How many people can say they're still close to a dozen childhood friends? And when we're together, there is no BS between us. We work in different fields: law, engineering, sales, law enforcement, technology, government, and more. No one is allowed to brag except about their children, and now grandchildren.

We're not sure what we'll do when we all turn seventy in 2020. I guess we need to find something that rhymes with "Social Security" or "retirement."

chapter 4
The Greatest Generation Redux

My mom passed away on February 6, 2005. I watched her die. Nine years earlier, I had watched my dad die.

I suppose it was good that I was there for both of them. They both went quietly, and I guess that's a blessing. But I'll never know what my dad or mom was thinking as they passed. Were they afraid? Were they at peace? Were they angry? Did they see me? Did they even know I was there? Did I give them any comfort in the end?

My mom was a quadriplegic. She fell walking the dog in 1970 and crushed her spine. She lay on the ground for hours before someone finally found her. She lived as a quad for thirty-five years and inspired everyone she ever met. Depression and self-pity were entirely foreign to her. And she had no tolerance for those who felt sorry for themselves.

My dad was a highly decorated army officer. After twenty years, he retired as a full colonel: the first full colonel from officer's candidate school after World War II and the youngest full colonel in the army at the time. He enlisted as a buck private in 1941, just months before Pearl Harbor. He fought in Korea, one of the bloodiest wars of our time. A true war hero.

Tom Brokaw described their generation as the greatest we've ever known. While I'm not sure if that's truth or hyperbole, I do know that my parents were the greatest duo I ever knew. They were a combination of George and Gracie, Ralph and Alice, and Ricky and Lucy. They were compassionate yet demanding. They pushed me to achieve. They had no patience for excuses. They insisted that I never look down on anyone. They taught me to respect God and authority. They let me grow. They made me laugh. They let me cry.

And they both battled their own private demons.

Dad was an alcoholic. He beat it after years of abusing himself. But despite all those years, the pain he gave is long forgotten, when measured against the love he gave. It's easier to remember all the good he brought to the family and taught us.

My dad didn't have a wake or funeral. I had him laid out in a funeral home, but only my brother and I bid him farewell. He was cremated and his ashes were scattered in a cemetery in New Jersey. Mom told me that's how he wanted it. I was never quite sure if that was true, but I honored her wishes. To this day, I miss the opportunity to have said goodbye in the company of his friends.

We had a wake for Mom. She was cremated and her ashes were scattered where my Dad's were scattered. I was overwhelmed by the number of people who came to Mom's wake. A true tribute to the inspiration she brought to so many people. A fitting farewell. I was honored to deliver her eulogy.

I hope and pray my children will look upon my life as I have upon the life and love of my parents. If I can leave them with that legacy, I will have accomplished what my mom and dad would have wanted—indeed expected—from me.

May God rest their souls.

Here's what I said at my Mom's funeral:

There are a lot of clichés used at times like this. We're here not to mourn, but to celebrate. Don't have sorrow for the loss but rejoice in her life. We know them all. But if there were ever a time when all those clichés were valid, it's tonight. Mom wouldn't want it any other way. In fact, if she were here right now, she'd probably wonder why everyone is making such fuss about her latest setback. Because I'm sure that's all it is to her. Just another challenge to overcome. And there's no doubt in my mind that she's dancing with my dad right now, finally freed from her wheelchair.

There are many people we need to thank for their many years of friendship and support for my mom and dad. Freda, Sandy, Rosa, and, of course, my sister from another mother, Louise. Louise was not only my mom's nurse, friend, and family member for more than twenty years, but she also took care of my dad, and as I was reminded the other day, my grandmother.

Thank you to all of you.

Not many people know just how rich and challenging my mom's life was. In many ways, it explains her tenacity and adventurous attitude. My "No Holds Barred Mom."

When she was in her late teens, she was run over by a car in Rutherford, New Jersey, where she grew up. She fractured her skull and broke her back. Doctors doubted she'd survive. But they didn't know that something as simple as fractured skull or broken back were a cakewalk for Mom.

She attacked rehab, recovered, and went on to become a registered nurse, and on November 8, 1941, at the age of 25, married my dad, then a newly recruited private in the Army, awaiting his duty station assignment.

And boy did their lives change just a month later on December 7, 1941, when the Japanese attacked Pearl Harbor.

Near the end of World War II, she accompanied my dad to a station assignment in Hawaii. Because she was a registered nurse, she and my then infant brother were allowed to accompany him. She volunteered as a nurse in the local hospitals and cared for the many wounded from the war. I can only imagine the horrors she saw in those years. Yet it never brought her down. No doubt she made many a soldier appreciate life even in their darkest moments.

Later, while my dad served in Korea, she stayed home in New Jersey with my brother, sister, and me. She continued working as a nurse. In fact, I was born while my dad was in Korea. I've no doubt it was not an easy time as a war-time mother bringing up three children without a father at hand for nearly two years.

And when we were stationed in Japan, Mom again rejected the stay-at-home life and started a nursery school, taking in kids from all over the Post. As if the three of us weren't already enough.

When my Dad retired from the Army in 1960—by then a full colonel—and took a job with ITT, Mom still wouldn't slow down. Instead of relaxing in retirement, she enrolled in Rutgers University and earned certification as a sanitarian, later became the public health nurse and sanitarian for Westwood. I was always convinced that she'd really gotten her training as a sanitarian dealing with my room while I grew up. Clearly, there were unknown species plentiful in that environment. And as my wife, Carol Ann, will tell you, our son, Josh, certainly continued that tradition.

It all seemed a charmed life. A caring nurse, the wife of a highly decorated Army officer turned successful businessman, and looking ahead to retirement now that the youngest of her children—me—was finally off to college and out of the roost.

But that all changed on January 1, 1970—a cold afternoon when she took our dog, Snitzel, for a walk. Snitzel was our small dachshund, or as my daughter, Andrea, likes to say, a wiener dog. As if there weren't already enough defining moments in her life and in the lives of everyone she knew or would come to know, that moment in the woods around the house would have crushed anyone else.

No one is sure exactly how she fell. Perhaps she slipped on ice. She also speculated that the injuries she'd suffered so many years earlier when she was hit by a car just caught up with her and she lost her balance. Regardless, she fell and lay on the cold ground for hours before she was finally found.

And so she began life as a quadriplegic.

I got my first inkling of how she planned to face that challenge when I visited her one day at St. Alban's Naval Hospital in Queens. She was in a ward with other patients who had suffered severe traumatic injuries, some of them returning wounded from Viet Nam. She lay in a contraption that looked like the wheel hamsters spin in cages. She was wired everywhere. And in considerable pain. As I sat there, not knowing what to say, she asked me what was the matter. I told her I didn't understand why this happened to her. How she could possibly get through it all? She shook her head—one of the few things that still moved. She told me to look around at the others. Many near death. Others in comas. Still others with little to live for.

And then she said, "I can't complain. They're all worse off. So don't pity me. I'll be fine."

And oh how she didn't like to be pitied. Or fussed over. She wanted everyone to think she was just someone who sat down a lot.

When she later went to the Kessler Institute for rehab, she dove into a brutal regimen. She tried everything she could to walk again. She exercised her arms and legs through excruciating pain to get some semblance of movement and control. Despite all the bad news and the reality that she'd never walk again or be able to take care of herself, she never lost her spirit and determination. Instead of being defeated, she just adjusted her attitude and tried a different direction. She was determined to be in control. Within weeks, she demanded an electric wheel chair. I remember the staff telling me the story of the first day she drove it. She went screaming down the hallway, totally out of control, damn near ran over everyone, and crashed into the wall. When they all ran to help her, she looked up and said, "Big deal. It's not like I'm going to hurt myself." That's when the folks at Kessler gave her the title "Bitch on Wheels."

She got on with her life. She became active in Hospice. Counseled others in similar situations. Became an advocate. Got out and did the shopping. Supervised the cooking. Even this past Christmas, we received the annual homemade cookies. In fact, her van was designed so she could maneuver her chair into the passenger side. In truth, she's always been in the driver's seat.

My friend, Bruce Burgess, wrote this about her:

"Without getting too mushy [he knows better], your mom has always had a special place in my heart, and was truly one of the most inspirational and heroic people that I have ever known. She was always positive, always had a fun or encouraging word, and always had a strong, upbeat, and almost unfathomably optimistic view of life.

The most telling quote of hers is a life benchmark: 'Everything always works out for the best.' This from a woman who endured horrendous back injuries that left her paralyzed and in a wheelchair for the rest of her life.

I have told that Rhoda Wood Story a hundred times over the years, especially to my children, and anyone else who might be in need of an attitude fix, an uplifting pat on the back, or facing some personal crisis.

Her quote, I tell them, should not only be appreciated for its obvious 'upbeat' content, but should also be measured by Mrs. Wood's incredible strength of spirit, tenacity, and her unfailing belief that in the end, all would indeed, turn out for the best.

Despite her circumstances, she never allowed pity to gather at her doorstep; she would never accept it from others, nor from herself.

If I could pass on to my children just a fraction of her magic positive attitude, her incredible strength of will, or her unfailing belief that everything ultimately works out for the best, I would consider that a wonderful legacy.

Her gift was to remind us all that we should be grateful for the life we are given, in whatever form it may come to us; and that we need to recognize just how much her positive spirit did to brighten the world around us."

I couldn't say it better than that.

Still another friend wrote:

"I will always remember those trips to visit your mom in rehab. She never talked about her condition but only wanted to know what the Boys were up to. She took great pleasure and interest in our early adult lives. I always think of the time we crashed at your house in Lincroft after your parents moved. Your mother and father welcomed us with open arms despite a little alcohol abuse on our part and then they made that awesome breakfast the next day. What your mom endured in her lifetime and how she handled it will always be an inspiration to all of us."

Always supportive, the word "no" was rarely in her vocabulary. Even when I went to her and asked if I could take my car—an old Rambler—paint people's names all over it, and drive it around Rutherford for 24 straight hours, swapping drivers throughout the night. Not only did she say yes to the Wood Rambler Marathon, but set up the house as driver central, ready with food, beds, and support throughout the 24 hours.

It was when we lived in Rutherford that I joined DeMolay, the Masons' youth organization. My mom always encouraged me to join just about anything that had other people breathing. She was the ultimate networker, forever pushing her children out front, encouraging us to be part of the community.

When I was installed as the grand master of my local chapter, the installation service included my reading a passage about mothers that is particularly appropriate today. Just as Mom was there to hear it then, I'm sure she's listening again now. And while the message is one from a son, it has equally poignant meaning for daughters as well. I had to memorize it then. But that ability is long gone, so sorry, Mom, but I'll have to read it this time.

It goes like this:

"For my purpose now, this Altar is dedicated to our mothers whose love never fails. You may rise to positions of great influence in commercial, political or professional life, but you can never reach the heights of your mother's secret hopes for you. You may sink into the lowest depths of infamy and degradation but never below the reach of her love. The memory of it will always stir your heart. There is no man so entirely base, so completely vile, so utterly low that he does not hold in his heart a shrine sacred and apart for the memory of his mother's love.

As a poet wrote:
Were I to draw you a picture of love divine,
It would not be that of a stately angel
With a form that is full of grace,
But a tired and toil-worn mother
With a grave and tender face.

It was your mother who loved you before you were born—who carried you for long months close to her heart and in the fullness of time took God's hand in hers and passed through the valley of shadows to give you life.

It was she who cared for you during the helpless years of infancy and the scarcely less dependent years of childhood. As you have grown less dependent, she has done the countless, thoughtful, trouble healing, helpful and encouraging things which somehow only mothers seem to know how to do."

That was my mom. And as she always said, "Don't worry, everything always works out for the best." So please leave tonight lifted by her spirit and ready to enjoy life to the fullest no matter what challenges you might face. That would be the way she'd want us all to honor her memory.

If we could all live the life of my mom and have her spirit of caring and loving, we'd all be better people.

chapter 5
Alcoholics Unanonymous

When my mom became a quadriplegic, my dad was devastated. Already a heavy drinker, he went off the deep end after Mom's accident. By the time I'd arrived home from college the afternoon of her accident, he was as drunk as could be. He stayed that way for months until I called Alcoholics Anonymous for help.

AA is an amazing yet frightening organization. With one phone call, they went into high gear. I was instructed to be at home on a particular night to wait for them to arrive. They told me to get my dad aggravated so he'd be emotional when they arrived.

"What are you going to do?" I asked.

"Don't worry. We'll do what's best for your dad."

On the night assigned, I purposefully got into an argument with Dad. He was drunk, so getting him angry wasn't hard. I also knew he'd never get violent, so I felt safe in pushing him.

When the doorbell rang, my stomach dropped. I had no idea what would happen next.

I answered the door and in walked three men. Dad immediately recognized one of them. He was an old friend and an AA member. I had no idea he'd be coming. But AA did their homework and I assumed it was part of their strategy to shock my dad by bringing someone he knew and throwing him off guard. It worked. My dad was immediately confused but still angry.

"What are you doing here?" he asked.

"Woody, we're here to help you." Woody was my dad's nickname.

I don't recall the conversation that ensued but by the end, Dad was taken away in a van and I was told they'd call me later. I asked where they were taking him. They told me they'd call.

I was shocked and not sure if I'd done the right thing. My dad was gone. My mom was in intensive care in a veterans' hospital. Could it get any worse?

The next day, AA called. They explained that Dad was in Paterson, New Jersey, at an AA facility on the corner of Straight and Narrow. No kidding. That was actually the name of the intersection. It was essentially a dry-up tank where he was held for a few days. They then transferred him to a camp in West Milford, New Jersey, for "treatment." While I wanted to know more, everything was vague. When I asked if I could talk to him or see him, I was told that would be a bad idea. They'd let me know when I could visit him at the "camp."

He was there for weeks. I eventually got to visit him together with my mom. While I'll never know what they did and my dad never told me, whatever it was, it worked. He came home sober and while he had a few relapses, AA was always there to bring him back to sobriety.

My mom eventually came home after mastering an electric wheelchair and adapting to a pulley system that helped her eat. Dad became her caretaker and a counselor in the AA community.

He stayed sober the rest of his life.

I remember when I was ten years old, I was walking with

my dad in San Francisco, when he suddenly stopped and looked down at me.

"Son," he said, "there's one thing in life I want you to remember."

I was mesmerized to think I was about to hear his wisdom after a lifetime of public service and heroism.

"Remember this. People are no damn good."

I didn't know how to respond. *People are no damn good?* That was what he wanted me to remember? I thought that was an awful thing to think. But as I would learn too many times, his words frequently turned out to be true.

One incident that proved his point occurred in the second semester of my sophomore year at University of Rhode Island. At that point, my dad was in the AA camp and Mom was in the hospital. I got a call from my dad's accountant, who was responsible for overseeing the finances of my dad's company, Wood-Warner Engineering Company, a firm in New York City that repaired elevators. My grandfather had founded it and my dad took it over after he retired from the army.

The accountant told me that there was no money left in the account and that he couldn't make payroll. He also said he couldn't pay the real estate taxes on the company's building, also owned by my dad. Wood-Warner was a company that had supported my parents and paid for their children's educations. While we didn't live like wealthy people growing up, the business had always provided what we needed with my mom working as well to supplement income.

But, the accountant told me, he had a solution. He offered me $10,000 to sell him the business and the building. He'd do all the paperwork. All I needed to do was get my dad to sign the documents. It would be simple and I'd have some money to boot.

I was shocked. First, that he would think I was an idiot who would fall for such a move after he'd been negligent in letting it get to that point. Worse, I knew he was aware of my parents' conditions. To take advantage of that after years of service and fees paid to him was an outrage. He was trying to steal the asset from under us for $10,000, at a time when my family was in desperate straits. The building itself had to be worth ten times that amount.

I declined his offer and immediately left Rhode Island and went to Wood-Warner, where I met my Great Uncle Alex, the shop foreman my grandfather had hired to run the shop and who my Dad had kept on. When I told him what happened, he was irate.

So we worked out a plan. We discovered the problem was my dad hadn't sent out invoices in months. He had been too drunk too often to tend to the business. And the accountant sat back and watched, waiting for his moment.

Alex and I prepared invoices, I bought a suit, and I started visiting customers asking for payment. While some were shocked to see a twenty-year-old asking that invoices be paid, most understood and made at least partial payments, even for jobs that had been closed. The business was saved.

Eventually, my brother left his job at General Electric and took over Wood-Warner. Although the company went out of business years later, it continued to support Mom and Dad under my brother's leadership.

To this day, that dose of the real world of greed and conniving reminds me of the wisdom of my dad's words, "Remember, people are no damn good." While I'd revise it to "Remember, at times, people are no damn good," it's a lesson worth remembering.

chapter 6
Sophie and Eman Prois

I never knew my paternal grandmother. My paternal grandfather died when I was three and I have no memory of him.

My first memory of my maternal grandparents is when I was ten. My dad had just retired from the army and we had moved to Rutherford, where my grandparents lived most of their lives since immigrating to the United States. My grandmother came from Romania and my grandfather from Germany. Although my parents' generation may have been accurately described as part of Brokaw's Greatest Generation, I believe they didn't hold a candle to their parents and what they went through, particularly those who immigrated to the United States at the turn of the twentieth century when the horror of World War I was looming.

My grandfather, Eman Prois, was from Germany. He came to America just before World War I. I don't know much about his life in his homeland. I was told he was an architect and that some great buildings bear his imprint. But that may have been nothing more than a myth my parents wanted me to believe. Years ago, my brother and I tried to trace his journey but could not find any immigration records. For all we know, he may have been an illegal alien. But if anyone was a dreamer as those we talk about today, my grandad was one of them.

When he arrived, he couldn't speak any English, so he couldn't get a job as an architect. He turned to commercial art. Among the things he did was paint state flags. To this day, flags he painted are in a museum in Rutherford. I still have some of his paintings and artwork. He was very good at his craft.

He was also a gardener, wine maker, and pipe smoker. I remember all of that well and can still recall the smells that permeated his house on Washington Avenue. His yard had apple, cherry, and beech trees. He grew rhubarb and other vegetables. During World War II, he and my grandmother tended to the town's Victory Garden, helping to feed those in need. My grandmother preserved all the fruits in the cellar. I remember them well too.

My fondest memory of my grandfather was his teaching me how to play chess. Chess was a game he loved, and his passion for it was unequaled. He was not a gentle teacher. He was tough and very critical when I made a poor move. I'll never forget how he stressed that I had to think multiple moves ahead if I ever hoped to win. On a number of occasions, he'd write down the moves he anticipated I'd make. Then when he beat me, he'd show me the paper. I don't recall him ever being wrong. When I asked him how he could possibly know what I was going to do when I didn't even know, he'd smile. "I don't know what moves you're going to make. I know what moves I'm going to make. And then I know how you'll react to every one of those moves. So it doesn't matter what you do. It only matters what I do. When you learn that, you'll know how to win."

That lesson still sits with me to this day as a great lesson in negotiating. Know where you want to go and make your moves in a way that can anticipate the reaction of your opponent. Lull them into a sense that they're in control when they're not. Move by move, bring them to the conclusion you want. Never rush. Patience is the key to success.

When I turned thirteen, he gave me a chess set he hand carved. I treasure it to this day.

After years of tutelage under my grandad, I finally beat him.

He never played me again. At first, I thought he was bitter about losing. Now I realize he had done his job. He wasn't really teaching me chess at all. He was teaching me how to succeed; how to get people to do what I want them to do. Once I'd learned that lesson, my classes were done.

Eventually, chess lost its allure to me. But I did teach it to my son. My daughters had no interest. Josh still plays to this day. And on the rare occasion he and I play, he beats me in record time. Maybe what he learned from me is a small part of why today he's a successful business negotiator. It's too bad he never got to know my grandad. They would have liked one another.

My grandmother Sophie, née Sophie Sandover, was less subtle.

In their home, pictures of my brother, sister, and me were on the wall. We always knew when she was mad at one of us when our picture was gone. That forced us to ask, "Grandma, what did I do?"

And she'd tell us in no uncertain terms. Then she'd put our picture back on the wall.

My brother and I were able to trace her ancestry and immigration through Ellis Island. I remember well the email I got from my brother.

"Doug, check out the attachment. It's the immigration papers for Grandma when she came to the United States with her mother and sister. Look at the entry under the column labeled *ethnicity*."

The entry read, "Hebrew."

I was flabbergasted. My grandmother was Jewish! I had no idea.

So I asked my mother about it.

"How did you find that out?" she asked, seemingly surprised that I'd made the discovery. I told her it was in the immigration records.

She told me that yes, Grandma was Jewish but that upon immigrating, her mother decided to bring her children up as Methodist although she herself never converted. She feared the persecution Jews were receiving in the United States and throughout the world and didn't want her children to experience the same. So my Aunt Charlotte and my mother were both brought up Methodist. And when my mom married my dad, my siblings and I were brought up as Episcopalians, my father's religion.

But technically, because my maternal lineage is Jewish, I'm Jewish.

Mazel tov. I can't wait for my Bar Mitzvah.

chapter 7
My (By Far) Better Half

I first met Carol Ann when I was in fifth grade after we moved from Hawaii to Rutherford. In class, we sat in alphabetical order and since her maiden name was Vogel, she sat immediately in front of me. As with any ten-year-old boy, I took great glee in aggravating her in class, including occasionally pulling on her blond hair. To put it mildly, she was no fan of mine.

As we ended fifth grade, I decided to extend an olive branch to her since we'd be in different homerooms in sixth grade and I didn't want her to leave with bad feelings. So I gave her one of the little plastic airplanes off my model of the U.S.S. *Forrestal*, a famous World War II aircraft carrier.

Now your first reaction to such generosity in fifth grade might not be overwhelming. But what if I told you that she kept it and still has it to this day? And what if I added that when our son, Josh, turned ten, I had him give her a little airplane from a new model of the U.S.S. *Forrestal*? Romantic? I think so.

Carol Ann and I drifted apart until our junior year in high school. I was sitting in the bleachers at a school dance when she walked across the gym floor. That was it. I was smitten. I knew she was dating a senior and my friends told me I had no chance if I asked her out. But I was determined.

When I finally got the nerve to call, Carol Ann's mother, Louise, answered the phone. I asked to speak to Carol. Her mother responded that there was no one named "Carol" who lived there and hung up. I remember staring at the phone and wondering if I had the right number. I checked. I had the right number. I called back. Her mother answered the phone. I asked for Carol. Her mother responded that there was no one named "Carol" but if I'd like to talk to "Carol Ann" she'd get her. And so began my very unique relationship with my mother-in-law. Talk about a protective matriarch! No one messed with Louise Vogel.

Shortly after our first date, I was invited to have dinner with Carol Ann's family. She had two sisters, Suzanne and Jonan. Her father, Fred, was an engineer who sold large machinery all over the world. More important, he was an engineer for the Manhattan Project, the United States program in Los Alamos, New Mexico, where they developed the atomic bombs that were dropped on Hiroshima and Nagasaki.

At dinner, I sat next to Carol Ann across from the two sisters. Fred and Louise sat at each end of the table.

Fred and Louise saw things differently and were not afraid to disagree with one another. The conversation was, to put it mildly, lively, quite unlike the calm atmosphere I experienced at home. There was simply no chance for any conversation beyond the bickering between Fred and Louise. The girls all sat in relative silence. Seeing no opening to speak, I decided to have some fun.

I took my paper napkin and secretly tore it in half on my lap. Carol Ann was suspicious but I gave her the "don't worry" look. Jonan or Suzanne noticed too and gave me the "Whatever you're doing, it's a bad idea" look. But I went on and took each half of my napkin and stuffed them into my ears while sporting a big smile because I thought it was hilarious.

Complete silence. I looked at Fred and I looked at Louise. Louise was clearly not amused. So I looked back at Fred. He just gave me a slight smile as if to say, "Hey kid, you got some balls." I looked back at Louise. I immediately learned that lasers can indeed emanate from a person's eyes and pierce through a skull. I took the napkins out of my ears and went back to my meal.

Carol Ann and I started dating in our senior year. We ended up both going to the University of Rhode Island and graduated in 1972. We got married in 1973 and moved to New Hampshire when I started law school. We now live in Wyckoff, New Jersey.

So we've been together for more than fifty years, married for forty-five. When we got married, the only thing I asked was that we never have Brussels sprouts or lamb in our household. She likes both and orders them when we go out. But she loved me enough when I asked and we've never had either in our home.

Someday perhaps she'll write her memoirs. I hope she's kind to me.

And at least we don't bicker like her parents did. Or at least not often.

chapter 8
Finding God

When I was seventeen and in my senior year of high school, my dad was transferred in a job he had with ITT and had to move to Eatontown, New Jersey, more than an hour away from Rutherford, where we'd lived for six years. I wanted to complete school at Rutherford High so I moved in with the Crosbys, friends of my parents.

Throughout my childhood, I was an acolyte at the local Episcopal Church and rose in the ranks to be the top dog. That allowed me to serve at weddings and funerals, where the tips were big. So the truth is I pretty much did it for the money. But the experience got me interested in becoming a minister. It seemed like a good way to help people. In my senior year, I applied to the Episcopal Seminary in New York.

The Crosbys were devout Catholics with close ties to the church. Mr. Crosby would come home each night from his job in New York City and was greeted at the door by Mrs. Crosby with a vodka gimlet in hand. On most nights, within minutes the doorbell rang and in came Father Bagley from the church. He got his gimlet and the two of them would sit in the living room, where I'd enjoy hearing them talk about their day, politics, and whatever came to their minds.

When Father Bagley learned of my thoughts about becoming a minister, he slowly but methodically grilled me about all sorts of religious issues. He said he wanted to be sure I truly had the calling to become a minister. After a couple of months, he concluded I did not and that I should pursue another walk of life. I knew he was right, and I eventually went to the University of Rhode Island.

At that point, I was pretty much agnostic or perhaps even an atheist. God was simply not a part of my life.

That all changed on December 21, 1981, the day my son, Joshua, was born.

As I stood in the delivery room watching my wife go through the agony and miracle of birth, I realized that such things are not a product of simple evolution from some single-celled amoeba. Josh was not the product of a fish turned land crawler turned ape, turned caveman, turned *homo sapiens*. He was a miracle far beyond that. So are my other two children, Meghan and Andrea, and my grandchildren, Sienna and Sydney. And so is much more around us. While scientists can tell us this all started with a big bang, I don't buy it. Our world and lives are too beautiful and amazing to have come about by some random explosion in space. A much bigger hand put this in motion. And although we're surrounded by unexplainable evil amidst the wonder, that is not reason to deny the teaching of religion in the Bible, Torah, or Quran.

When Josh was born, I was born again. Not as a zealous Bible-beating Christian, but as a quiet believer. On that day, I came to embrace a much higher power and I remain a believer today. How anyone who witnesses the birth of a child that they helped create can believe otherwise is a complete mystery to me.

chapter 9
A Bridge Too Far

College life in the late '60s and early '70s was deep into the Greek life. Being in a fraternity or a sorority was the on-ramp to a social life. The University of Rhode Island was no exception. Going Greek was the norm.

One of the big events at URI every year was the annual party to celebrate the new sorority sisters. And it was common for upperclassmen in fraternities to be the new sisters' dates for the fete. While I was dating Carol Ann at the time, she did not pledge a sorority. So in early 1970, at the behest of one of my fraternity brothers, I agreed to take a new sorority sister to the party as a blind date. The two of us got to the off-campus venue in Westerly, Rhode Island, in my Oldsmobile Dynamic 88, a behemoth car. For this story, we'll call my date Sally. That was not her real name.

What exactly happened to me at the party is still unknown to me and everyone who was with me, even Sally. The last thing I remember is going to the bar to get a drink early in the night. Everyone I later spoke to about the night agreed that when I went to get the drink, I was sober. What happened next is pieced together by the stories of others who were there in discussions over the next few days.

Sally said I told her I wanted to leave and the two of us drove off in the Olds. She said I was driving erratically by the time I got on Route 95 South on our way back to URI. As I drove, I apparently became more and more erratic and Sally asked me to pull over. After doing so, I walked into the woods, telling Sally that I needed to relieve myself. When I came back, she said I was disheveled, my glasses were gone, and my face was scratched. She speculated that I must have fallen.

At that point, a tractor trailer pulled over behind us and the driver asked if everything was OK. Sally said no and that she didn't want to get in my car. The truck driver offered a ride back to URI. As she was getting into the truck, I asked her to give me her glasses so I could see where I was going. She handed them to me and the two drove off.

Apparently, I got back in my car and continued down Route 95 and got off at an exit in Connecticut. Reconstructing the events from that moment paints a bizarre story.

At about 2:00 a.m., I drove into a small town and took out five guardrails and a telephone pole. From there, I drove the car off a bridge. It landed on its roof in the icy water. Through some miracle, however, I fell out of the car and onto the bridge. Some speculate that when I hit the telephone pole and the car flipped, the door must have opened and I fell out. In those days, no one wore seatbelts. In an ironic way, that may have saved my life.

I then walked to a house across the street and stepped onto the porch. The woman who lived there said I started knocking on her door asking for help. She stayed inside and called the police. When the woman didn't answer the door, I walked back across the street directly through the plate glass window of a Buick dealership, seriously cutting my head and face and bleeding profusely. I proceeded to sit in the front seat of a new car, apparently trying to start it. Thank God there was no key in the ignition.

At that point, the police arrived and took me into custody and off to the local hospital. As the front of my nose was being stitched back on, I awoke, and my memory restarted from there. But from the time I went to the bar at the party to the time I awoke at the hospital, I remember nothing.

As I awoke, a very grumpy overweight police sergeant was hovering over me. No doubt he was not pleased to be working at 4:00 a.m. He asked me my name. I told him. He showed me both my real and my fake ID. The drinking age was twenty-one, so like many undergraduates, I had a fake ID. He asked if the fake ID was mine. I said yes, still in a fog with no knowledge where I was or how I got there.

"Well young man, your fake ID is a violation of law that could land you in jail for five years. And your destruction of public and private property is a felony."

In all, I had over forty stitches to my head, lacerations all over my face and arms, and muscles severely pulled across my back. I could barely stand.

Despite my injuries, I was not admitted to the hospital but instead taken to the police station and placed in a cell. I was told I'd be charged with a number of crimes. I was never given any Miranda warnings, nor offered the chance to make a call. Just stuck in a cell.

At that point, I was in a panic. I still had no clue what happened. I didn't know where Sally was. I was told my car was being lifted out of the river by a crane. I feared they'd find Sally's body in it. Keep in mind that this happened at the same time Ted Kennedy left Mary Jo Kopechne to drown in a tidal channel on Chappaquiddick Island. I'd never been more afraid in my life.

As the sun rose, the shift changed and a young police officer arrived to run the desk. The sergeant left.

Leaning up against the bars of the cell, I called out to the desk officer, who I could see to my right. He walked over. He was not smiling.

"What do you want?"

"Officer, please let me out of this cell. I'll sit quietly in a chair but I don't belong in here."

This was the first time he'd looked at me. I suspect he thought he was looking at Frankenstein with all the stitches and cuts on my face and the filthy, bloodied clothes I was wearing. I guess he took some pity on me or figured I was in no shape to pose a flight risk.

"As long as you don't make trouble, I'll let you sit in a chair by the front desk."

As I sat there, the officer and I discussed what happened and he put a lot of the pieces together for me. I lamented how I had screwed up but never mentioned Sally. He told me not to worry; that it would all work out. At that point, I didn't believe him. Eventually, he asked me if I'd like to make a call. I called my sister, who lived in Rhode Island, and she quickly came to get me.

When she and my brother-in-law arrived, they were shocked at what they saw. I looked like shit. And felt worse. The officer told me I was free to leave with them as long as I signed out and promised to come back for any hearings. That was odd, since I'd been told I was going to be charged with some serious crimes yet was never formally arrested or booked. But I wasn't going to argue.

As we were leaving, the officer asked if I'd like to see the car. I said yes, wondering what I'd find there. The car was sitting in a lot by the river, the roof crushed. I cautiously looked inside, where I saw Sally's glasses. Keep in mind I had no memory of what happened to her. The officer saw them too and asked, "Whose glasses are those?" I quickly grabbed them, put them on, and said, "Mine." He looked at me oddly, since the glasses had rhinestones and pointed corners, but I guess he dismissed it as just another weird college student accessory.

On the road home, my sister asked me about the glasses. I told her they weren't mine. They belonged to the girl who was with me and I had no idea where she was. My brother-in-law nearly drove off the road.

When we finally arrived at my fraternity house, a dozen of my brothers were sitting in the reception area and upon seeing me were obviously relieved. I later learned that Sally reported what happened and they were driving all over the state looking for me.

I hired a lawyer to handle the case.

I asked Sally if she'd like to go out again and promised I wouldn't be driving. She declined. Smart.

But that's not the end of the story.

Months later I was home in New Jersey. Collecting the mail, I noticed an envelope from the police department in Connecticut where I'd spent the night. I opened it with trepidation, fearing the worst. In it was an unsigned note that simply read, "You owe me. Good luck."

Accompanying the note was my fake ID cut into pieces. I can only speculate that the officer who took pity on me sent it. I'll never know. I've never asked.

I eventually pleaded guilty to a traffic violation, a charge less than a misdemeanor, on condition that I pay all the damages to the guardrails, telephone pole, and auto dealer. I gladly did so. Shortly after that, my lawyer petitioned to have the entire file expunged. His motion was granted.

Net result, I was a college student who really screwed up, but God and an angel were on my shoulder and made sure that what could have been a tragic story was a lesson on being aware of what is around you. It's the reason I always caution my kids that being in the wrong place, wrong time, can change your life. I was given a second chance. Most people are not.

I was once asked if I'd like to undergo hypnosis to find out if I could recall that six- or seven-hour period of amnesia. The answer is no. I never want to relive those moments.

chapter 10
LBLS—Life before Law School

It's relatively safe to say that before I went to law school, there wasn't a party I missed if I knew about it. Nor were there many bars I skipped. As my dad told me years later when I became a lawyer, "Son, you're the first Wood who could actually pass a bar."

So I had fun. And my grades reflected it. In my first semester at URI, I got a 1.9 GPA. Second semester, I raised it to a whopping 2.1. Then I hit my first semester, sophomore year. I "earned" a GPA of 1.4—which meant probation. That woke me up. Sort of. While I got more serious about my studies and switched from engineering to political science, I didn't stop partying, eventually graduating with a 2.6 GPA. Nothing impressive.

In my senior year, I took the Law School Admission Test (LSAT) and scored very high. I had the kind of score that places like Harvard looked for. So naturally I assumed I'd have an easy ride into a great law school. Still, I wasn't crazy. I knew my GPA would probably keep me out of Harvard or Yale but figured everyplace else was fair game. I applied to twelve top law schools. NYU, Virginia, William & Mary, Georgetown, and others.

As I approached graduation, one rejection after another arrived. Eventually, all twelve rejected me.

I needed a job.

I eventually landed at an insurance company as a claims adjuster.

Working for an insurance company as a claims adjuster was a real eye-opener about the real world of business and insurance. I learned quickly that making decisions was more important than necessarily making the right decisions. As a judge once told me, progress is made by getting things just about right but not perfect.

My first inkling of my new world came when I moved into a new apartment and applied to get a telephone line from AT&T. In 1972, you had to ask AT&T, a monopoly and only source for a phone, to install a line. It was a pretty detailed application that I assumed was just a formality.

I completed the application and made the mandatory appointment with an AT&T representative, a woman who seemed very nice when I first met her. She had a grandmother's look with white hair.

After some pleasantries, she asked me what I did for a living.

"I'm a claims adjuster."

"You're despicable."

Huh? I thought. Why am I despicable? All I want is a frickin' telephone.

"What do you mean? I don't understand."

"I was denied coverage in an insurance claim. I know what you do. You just deny people money they're owed. You don't care."

I suddenly realized claims adjusters were no more loved than used car salesmen. And I hated car salesmen. The thought of being in the same club made the excitement that I had a job in insurance a wee bit less endearing. But I slogged on.

"I'm sorry you feel that way. That's not how I look at my job. But more importantly, I need the phone. Can we take care of that?"

"I'll put your request in the system and we'll get back to you."

I wanted to suggest what she could do with herself but decided it was better to be polite.

"When do you think I'll hear?"

She replied, with the tone of the nightmare teachers I remembered in grade school, "Like I said, I'll put it in the system."

I got the phone a month later.

With that lovely endorsement from the phone company, I began my new job.

After six weeks of training outside Philadelphia on the art of insurance investigation, I was assigned to the East Orange, New Jersey, office.

I dove into investigating cases using all the skills I'd learned in training. I staked out locations to find witnesses. I took photos of accident sites. I interviewed witnesses. I wrote reports. I analyzed medical reports. I talked to doctors. I verbally beat up plaintiffs' lawyers.

But after one month, I still hadn't settled a case. I was called into my manager's office.

"What's the matter? How come you're not settling cases?"

"I'm investigating them. I'm trying to make sure I have all the facts and can determine if we should deny or pay and if so, how much."

"That's nice but that's not what I want. I want you to move the cases along. You need to settle them. We don't want to carry big reserves. You're overworking the files. Start closing them."

I was crestfallen. All that education in investigating seemed for naught.

So I did exactly what I was told to do. I settled. A lot.

And before I knew it, I was promoted to a trial adjuster and started working with the lawyers in court, sitting beside them at counsel's table. My job was to analyze cases going to trial, monitor those that went to court, and make sure, above all else, that the insurance company didn't get hit with a big verdict. By then, I knew what that meant. Settle.

I only allowed one case—a routine car accident—to go to a jury. We represented the driver of one car and another insurance company represented the driver of the other car. The plaintiff was the passenger in our insured's car. The other driver ran a red light and plowed into the passenger door of our insured's car. No one denied those facts. Nonetheless, I told the adjuster for the other insurance company that if he'd settle the case paying the majority of the claim (since his driver ran the red light), I'd throw in some money to get rid of it. Amazingly, he refused, telling me that the jury would find the two drivers equally responsible to the plaintiff. After about an hour's deliberation, the jury came back with the verdict holding the other driver 100 percent liable and our driver off the hook. It made me a hero.

Two other cases are also worth remembering.

In one, an electrician was working on an electrical panel. He dropped his screwdriver. It hit the panel, causing it to arc with an electrical charge that gave off more heat than the sun. It instantly vaporized his pants, causing serious injury. So he sued the makers of the pants because they advertised them as flame resistant. At trial, we proved that the fabric in the pants passed every federal rule on claiming flame resistance and that no fabric existed that could have withstood the heat generated by the electrical arc he caused when he dropped his screwdriver.

As the insurance company lawyer put it to me, "We've got this one. There's no way we're on the hook. Don't settle." He was right on the law.

The plaintiff's attorney then produced photos taken in the emergency room and asked that they be placed in evidence and shown to the jury. I immediately grabbed the insurance company lawyer's arm and said, "You can't let in those photos. They're unbelievably disgusting."

He stood and objected. He was overruled. The plaintiff's attorney started passing the photos out to the jury. What they saw wasn't all that important. It was what they didn't see. They didn't see his penis or testicles because they were gone. Burned off.

I told the attorney to ask for a recess. I took the plaintiff's lawyer outside and settled for more than $1 million. There was no way I could let that go to the jury.

In another case, a drunk was driving on the New Jersey in his convertible late at night when he lost control near a construction site, hit an abutment, and was thrown from the car. Experts estimated he must have been driving over eighty miles per hour through a stretch of road marked with a forty-five mile per hour limit. None of those facts were in dispute.

After hurtling about a hundred feet through the air, he impaled himself on a metal post like those used to mount caution signs. The post went right though his chest. He also lost an eye at some point between the ejection and landing.

Somehow, the guy lived.

He sued the construction company for improper maintenance

of the construction site by allowing the sign post to remain. Somehow, his lawyer believed he had a case of negligence when his drunken client crashed his car, flew a hundred feet, and landed on the post. The insurance company lawyer insisted it was a "no-liability case" and that we'd win at trial. He was right on the law.

At trial, the plaintiff's lawyer asked him on the stand what his life was like since the crash. The first thing he mentioned was the difficulty he had with all the scars on his chest and inability to control muscle spasms from being impaled. So his lawyer asked him to take off his shirt and show the jury.

Out went my hand to the insurance company's lawyer, "You can't let him do that. It will be unbelievably disgusting."

He stood and objected. He was overruled.

Then the lawyer for the plaintiff threw us a curve. Instead of instructing him to remove his shirt, he asked, "Is there anything else?"

"Yes," his witness replied. "I have trouble with my artificial eye."

Before we could do a thing, he removed the eye, holding it in his hand. It was clearly a setup.

The jury gasped. The insurance company lawyer jumped up and objected, saying this was extreme prejudice and the judge should declare a mistrial.

The judge ordered that the jury be removed from the courtroom. When the jury was out, the judge told us he did not see the incident with the eyeball as prejudicial enough for a mistrial. He told us he'd simply instruct the jury to take it within the context of the overall case. I had no idea what that meant. And if I didn't, I knew the jury would never understand that.

The judge then asked for the witness to remove his shirt so the judge could see the injury. When he did so, my worst suspicion was confirmed. It wasn't just unbelievably disgusting. It was grotesque. Not only did it look like a roadmap with all the scars but the spasms, obviously controlled by the witness, were sure to make the jurors sick to their stomachs, eyeball in "context" or not.

I grabbed the lawyer's arm, "Make another objection to prevent the plaintiff from showing himself to the jury. This is nuts. Between the eye and the shirtless monstrosity, they won't give a damn that he was drunk."

The lawyer made the objection. The court denied it and told the bailiff to bring back the jury.

I asked for a recess. I was given fifteen minutes.

I took the plaintiff's attorney outside and settled for almost $1 million. I knew better than to let the case go to a jury.

After about six months as a trial adjuster, I was once again promoted and assigned to work on workmen's compensation claims made by longshoremen. That meant I went to the seaport in Newark to interview burly longshoremen and try to find witnesses who would rat on the injured union brothers. Yeah, right.

It was considered the toughest job in the company but I had apparently made a great impression on the higher-ups. That impression was supported by the fact that I spent the insurance company's money like a drunken sailor. But that wasn't the only measure of success. What mattered is that I never lost a trial and never settled a case above the reserve.

Having been promoted to trial adjuster, and having accompanied the lawyers to court, monitored cases, and settled them if the lawyers feared a bad verdict, I resolved to try to get into law school again. I applied to twelve more law schools, this time closer to the bottom of the heap. Schools like Suffolk, New England, Salmon P. Chase, and eight other barely known institutions. I took the LSAT again and did even better. I was confident I'd be a shoo-in.

And then the rejections started flowing in. One by one, my dreams were being shattered. I finally ended up being rejected by every one of them. I now had twenty-four law school rejections under my belt.

But something happened. Out of nowhere, I got a postcard from a new law school in Concord, New Hampshire, the Franklin Pierce Law Center. Brand new, and only provisionally accredited by the American Bar Association. I filled out the postcard and mailed it in. What did I have to lose?

Carol Ann and I got engaged in June 1973, found an apartment, and bought some furniture. Our wedding date was set for August 25, and planning was complete. Carol Ann got a great job at a bank and in July, I had an offer from Chubb & Sons at a better salary than I'd ever make at the insurance company I was working for. We were well on our way to a new life.

Then a few days before I was planning on giving notice to my employer, and the same day Carol Ann would attend a surprise wedding shower, I got a telephone call from Robert Viles, the associate dean of Franklin Pierce. He invited me to come to the school for an interview. I barely remembered even applying, and at that point in my life's plans I had pretty much dropped any idea of becoming a lawyer. I told him I was getting married in four weeks, taking a new job, and simply didn't have time to come up for an interview. He responded, "OK, let's do it now on the phone." So we talked for about an hour. At the end of the interview, he said, "OK, you're in." I literally responded, "In what?" He laughed and said, "You're in law school, assuming you still want to become a lawyer."

That night, as I drove Carol Ann to her wedding shower, I gave her a bigger surprise than she'd bargained for.

When I finally gave the insurance company notice telling them I was going to law school, they told me I was making a big mistake. They even had some honchos come down from the home office with charts showing me how I'd financially do much better staying with a career in insurance than I'd ever do as a lawyer.

Thank God they were wrong.

~~asshole~~
attorney

chapter 11
Franklin Pierce Law Center

The Franklin Pierce Law Center (now part of the University of New Hampshire) was located on Mountain Road in East Concord, New Hampshire. On either side were cow farms. The facility itself was a former bull breeding farm, complete with a silo and small rooms where bulls were encouraged to have their way with heifers. The barn with the silo was converted into the library. The breeding stalls became study rooms. A large classroom was added, as well as some offices. The house on the farm became the dean's residence. While cows were not enrolled, they constantly wandered over from the adjoining farms, occasionally requiring that we take a break from class and chase them away. Fly strips hung from the rafters to catch the flies that loved to be near the wandering cows.

The school itself was founded by Robert Rines, a famous but somewhat maverick patent lawyer whose passion in life was chasing the Loch Ness monster. He believed the U.S. patent system was anti-inventor and deplored the fact that patent lawyers were educated to favor corporate America looking for fast profits rather than the nurturing of inventors and innovators. Rines put his money where his mouth was, and in 1973 founded a law school with a laser focus on intellectual property law and changing the system. To this day, Bob Rines is considered one of the most innovative patent lawyers and educators law schools have ever seen (he passed away in 2009).

But he was a wee bit eccentric. His mission to find the Loch Ness monster and to export his intellectual property ideas to foreign lands kept him away from Concord a good deal of the time. But he really wasn't the professorial type, so we didn't really miss him. We did enjoy, however, his annual lecture on the latest success in finding the monster. It was very entertaining.

The school was run by Bob Viles, an equally interesting man. Viles was not an intellectual property lawyer at all. He came to Franklin Pierce after stints at the University of Kentucky College of Law and as a research director for the U.S. Commission on the Bankruptcy Laws. And now he was running a law school that couldn't care less about the financial world unless it helped fund sensible intellectual property laws. But Bob Rines knew he needed a real educator as the lead dog, and his choice of Viles was brilliant.

I was part of the first class. We had no upperclassmen. To solve that problem, the school hired Joe Dickinson, a Root Tilden Scholar from New York University School of Law, to fill the role. He also taught legal writing.

To round out the faculty, the school added Dick Hesse, an expert on the Constitution; Dane Buck, a New York tax lawyer who said he wanted to see leaves instead of asphalt; Don Simpson, the just-retired dean of Suffolk Law School; and Tom Fields, a professor and former patent examiner. Like Viles and Dickinson, he had a law degree from New York University.

Before law school, my only mentor was my dad. In law school, I was blessed with many. Joe Dickinson, after I handed in my first writing assignment, told me I'd better get serious about my education or get out and find something else to do. Dick Hesse taught me how to think critically and understand core principles in legal jurisprudence. Don Simpson taught me to get to the point quickly lest I get thrown out of his office. Tom Fields inspired me to care about intellectual property and the care and feeding of the innovators who make this country great. Rines showed us all that following dreams was not inconsistent with making a difference.

Rines was also a very practical man despite his dalliances with frivolity. I will never forget one classroom question. Before a class of about fifty students, he asked, "You're in a room. On one side of the table, you sit with the person who hired you as their lawyer. On the other side of the table sits another lawyer and the person who hired him. You're there negotiating a deal. How many clients are in the room?"

We were all confused. What kind of trick question was this? One person responded, "One. The only client I should care about is the one who hired me. I need to be his advocate." Another student suggested, "None until I get paid." A few more inane answers followed. I chose not to contribute an answer when I didn't have a clue what he was looking for.

Looking at all of us with feigned disdain, he said, "There are three. Your client, the other lawyer's client, and the deal. You're in the room for a purpose shared by those two clients: to get the deal done. So you have to look upon the deal as the third client. Because if you don't do the deal, you failed to achieve the goal you came into the room to accomplish." I've never forgotten that advice. Advocacy is one thing, but when it becomes destructive of the mutual goals of clients—mine and the other lawyer's—we fail.

But it was Viles whom I came to most admire. And my special relationship with him began on the third day of law school.

I was told he wanted to see me. Nervous, I arrived at the appointed time and sat across from him at a cluttered desk. I'd never met a man quite like Viles. He was well over six feet tall, lanky, and had one of the deepest voices I've ever heard. He sported a goatee and looked a lot like pictures we've seen of Abraham Lincoln.

"Mr. Wood," he said, "we have a small problem. You have not paid your tuition and you can't stay if you can't pay."

I felt as if a truck had hit me. Shit. I had quit my job, sold my furniture, moved to some Godforsaken state in the middle of nowhere with horrible weather. I had barely begun law school and I was about to be thrown out. I decided to tell him the truth.

"Dean Viles, I don't have the money. I only recently applied for a student loan but haven't heard back yet. You may recall that I was the last person admitted, just a few weeks ago."

"Well that's a hell of a thing." That expression would later become his trademarked way of responding to a perceived problem.

He opened his top desk drawer, removed his checkbook, wrote out a check to me for the full tuition, and handed it to me, saying, "Put this in your account and write a check to the school for the tuition. You can pay me back when you get the student loan."

Unbelievable.

And that was only the beginning of our relationship. From there, he not only taught me how to think like a lawyer but also why the law, despite all of its warts, works better here than anywhere else in the world. And when I was short of cash, he hired me to paint rooms in the law school and at his house. He encouraged me to write and pushed me to be on law review.

Years after I graduated, he asked me to join the board of trustees, which I would eventually chair for fifteen years. No single person did more to mold me into a lawyer than Bob Viles.

When he tragically drowned in 1999 off the coast of Brittany, where he was pulled under by strong ocean currents, I was devastated, and seriously questioned my faith. I cried for hours but then got to thinking what he'd say. And it came to me. "Well this is a hell of a thing." And I knew I'd be fine and needed to move on. It was my honor to deliver a eulogy at his funeral. I still miss him but am inspired by him whenever I face a tough situation. Viles and my mom ingrained me with optimism.

Always.

chapter 12
LALS—Life after Law School

By the time I'd finished law school, I was in the top rankings of my class, on the law review, and had glowing recommendations from my professors.

But I had no job. Graduating from a brand-new law school, despite how well I'd done, didn't open any doors. I was left with three choices: work with my brother-in-law in Rhode Island, where he practiced real estate law; enlist in the army and become a captain in JAG; or go to New York University and earn a master of law degree (LLM) in trade regulation. I knew I didn't want to be a real estate lawyer, so Rhode Island was out. And while the army offer was enticing, I'd had my fill of army life. So that was out. All that was left was paying to go to law school for another year and earning a second law degree. NYU won by default.

How different NYU was compared to Franklin Pierce! In Concord, the school atmosphere was warm and folks genuinely wanted to help one another succeed. At NYU, it was survival of the fittest. I hated it. When graduation came in May 1977, I didn't even bother to go to the ceremony. The school meant nothing to me.

But I do owe NYU a big thank-you for letting me be at the right place, right time. Fate gave me an opportunity that set me on the career path I enjoy today.

Once I saw how little I was enjoying NYU, I looked for a part-time job to get myself out of the Washington Square environment. Pinned up on the placement office billboard was an ad for a law clerk at Abeles, Clark & Osterberg. I had no idea what the firm did, and I didn't care. I wanted a job. I applied, interviewed with John Clark and Bob Osterberg, and got the job.

By pure luck, Abeles, Clark & Osterberg turned out to be the dream job that just about every law school student would kill for. The firm specialized in litigation for recording companies and music publishers. It was the heyday of rock 'n' roll, when labels gave bands just about anything they wanted. It was the age of the demands for unbelievably expensive album jackets and tour support, and when some bands wouldn't perform unless their M&Ms were the right color and a bottle of Jack Daniels was on the stage. Bands trashed hotel rooms on a whim. They didn't pay their taxes and had the IRS on their heels. They just didn't care and knew the labels would pay. And pay they did. It was a great practice. I got to hang out with rock stars most people only dreamed of meeting. The only problem was that many of them didn't like lawyers and treated us, particularly the new kid on the block like me, with clear disdain.

This was my first experience as a lawyer working with other lawyers and dealing with difficult clients. It was quite the rude awakening. Legal theory became secondary to practical solutions. Settling cases was primary. I began thinking I was back at the insurance company where facts gave way to a driving desire to settle cases and get the reserves off the books. Never mind who was really at fault.

When I started at the firm as a clerk, Julian Abeles was

gone. He'd died years earlier. John Clark was a former prosecutor. I remember the associate at the firm (there was only one) telling me how proud Clark was relating the story that on cross-examination he once gave a witness a heart attack. The witness died. I have no idea if the story is true. I found John Clark to be a kind and gentle man.

Bob Osterberg was a consummate litigator. Very strategic and creative. One of the best lawyers I ever knew. He's retired now, but in the '70s he was at the top of his game and almost legendary in his success. I learned more about the practical side of being a lawyer in the one year I worked with him than I did in four years of law school.

The cases the firm handled were groundbreaking. In one case, the firm sued ABC when the network aired *Monty Python's Flying Circus* with commercial breaks at all the wrong moments. As far as the creators of *Monty Python* were concerned, ABC butchered their work. They sued under a uniquely European concept known as *droit moral*—the rights of an artist to insist that anyone who uses their work respects its integrity. It had never before been recognized in the United States, but that didn't stop Osterberg. He developed a breach-of-contract theory and won at trial. Then he won when ABC appealed. To this day, *Gilliam v. American Broadcasting* is regarded as one of the groundbreaking cases in intellectual property law and the protection of an artist's inherent rights to his or her creations. And I was there to be part of it as a lowly law clerk.

In another case, the firm brought a suit against Earl Wilson Jr., when he used the musical score of the famous World War II classic the "Boogie Woogie Bugle Boy (of Company B)" in what Wilson claimed was a parody titled, "The Cunnilingus Champion of Company C" in the play *Let My People Come*.

At the hearing for an injunction to halt further use of the song, Osterberg told me to see if there were any older people hanging around the courthouse and tell them the Boogie Woogie Bugle Boy was going to be performed in court. (Last I spoke to him, he didn't remember those instructions, but I sure do.) I managed to find about a dozen oldsters in the halls and they helped pack the courtroom, already filled with seniors. Osterberg had a spinet piano installed in the courtroom. The judge was Irving Ben Cooper, a WWII veteran, obviously a fan of the song, and a bad draw for Wilson. In his typical theatrical manner, Osterberg first had "Boogie Woogie Bugle Boy" performed live for the judge and those gathered in the courtroom. No recording was going to be good enough. The courtroom was rocking! The seniors were bouncing to the music. So was Judge Cooper. Then Osterberg asked the actors from *Let My People Come* to perform their parody. Why they were foolish enough to do so I will never know, but they did. A bunch of long-haired hippies started to sing:

> He was the cunnilingus champion of company "C"
> A diddlie twat a diddlie twat.
> Lickety split he's in the army now, who's in the army now?
> I said the cunnilingus champion of company "C."
> Some say he came from Memphis maybe it was St. Jo.
> And how he learned to eat a pussy we'll never know
> The pressure from his lips was just amazingly strong
> His tongue could move much faster than us singin' this song
> A diddlie twat a diddlie twat a twat twat twat.

A did-dl-ie twat a diddlie twat oh twat twat twat.
He was some cunnilingus champion of company "C."

At first, those gathered in the courtroom didn't get it. After all, their average age was probably eighty and cunnilingus was as far from their minds as one could imagine. But by the time the cast got to "pussy," the audience figured it out and started booing. By the end of the performance, the booing drowned out the singers and Judge Cooper was pounding his gavel for order in the court. It was brilliant, and I thought I was in Hollywood. Needless to say, Osterberg got the judge to order the song be stricken from the play.

By the time of trial, Osterberg had developed an argument that Wilson's song was not a parody but merely an example of music stolen for sheer entertainment purposes. To be a parody, Osterberg argued, the new song needed to be a satire of the original. It needed to ridicule it in some way. It couldn't simply be a springboard for humor or pirated music. His argument not only won at trial but also on appeal. Today, *MCA Music v. Earl Wilson* is considered by many to be the pivotal case establishing the principles for a valid parody defense.

I served a subpoena on a famous rock 'n' roller while he was having lunch at the Plaza Hotel and had to run out of the restaurant when his friends stood and started chasing me. I went to clubs late at night to pick up the gate proceeds in paper bags to take home and return to the firm the next day so the money got paid to the IRS to satisfy a tax lien on the performer. I sat quietly while I watched one performer snort lines of cocaine while we interviewed him.

The biggest lesson I learned in my year with Abeles, Clark & Osterberg was that when the performers weren't footing the bill, they really didn't care what the lawyers thought. Some were downright antagonistic. We had instructions with regard to one band that we should not be in a room alone with them because they really hated lawyers.

But after a year, it got to be too much. The hours were brutal and I was genuinely concerned that I might become an alcoholic or drug addict. Or both. I sent my résumé to every intellectual property law firm in New York that I could find in a book called *Martindale-Hubbell*. In its day, *Martindale-Hubbell* was the bible of law firm directories. Today, it's essentially a relic of history because we have a host of digital directories other than that one. But in the '70s, that's all there was. And the two years it took to find a law school that would admit me had taught me that I couldn't be picky. I don't recall how many firms I solicited, but it was easily over one hundred.

Felix Kent, then a name partner at Hall Dickler Lawler Kent & Howley, called me to an interview. He later confessed that the real reason he called was because I'd done a summer clerkship between my second and third year of law school for JAG in Wurzburg, Germany. Kent was a World War II veteran who was stationed in Germany after the war to interrogate Nazis. Or something like that. I never quite understood what he did there but I knew it was serious stuff. He wanted to know what Wurzburg was like. I must have done well with the travelogue because he offered me a job as a copyright litigator, a natural extension of what I did at Abeles, Clark & Osterberg.

On September 14, 1977, I began anew in the firm's offices at 460 Park Avenue. I was a frickin' Park Avenue lawyer!

At first, however, I didn't work for Kent. He was not a litigator. I worked for Mel Fenster and Gerry Dickler. Fenster was a kind man who never applied much pressure. A real nice guy.

Dickler, on the other hand, was just plain mean and constantly critical. But he had clients like Georgia O'Keeffe, Jackson Pollock, and Lowell Thomas. And he represented Capital Cities Communications, a broadcaster with television stations in New York State. Cap Cities would later acquire ABC in a transaction that put Dickler into a footnote given his substantial stock holdings. I remember thinking that some day, I'd like to be a footnote in an annual report. Working for his clients was where I wanted to be, but that meant working with someone very befitting of the title of this book.

One afternoon, I was ordered into his office. With the door still open, he blew up and fired me, telling me to get out. I was done.

In shock, I went back to my office and started packing up my stuff. Kent walked in and asked me what I was doing. I told him, almost in tears, that Dickler just fired me. "Oh," said Kent. "Well you're hired back. Stop packing."

A few weeks later, Dickler stopped me in the hallway and asked me why I was still there. I walked into his office with him in tow, closed the door, and told him that I'd been hired back. I said I'd like to work with him again but only if he treated me with respect. He just stared at me, so I walked out. Within about a week, he asked me to work on a variety of matters for some of his most famous clients. Although I never did come to like the man, we respected one another and had a professional relationship. Working with Dickler taught me that you can work for an asshole attorney as long as you set up some parameters. And given all the assholes I've had to work with over the years, the lessons Dickler taught me were invaluable.

chapter 13
Hall Dickler Lawler Kent & Howley

On Halloween, October 31, 1985, my professional life was turned upside down. I'd been an associate in the advertising law group of Hall Dickler Lawler Kent & Howley for eight years. That morning, I was greeted with the announcement that David Carlin and Bill Marlow, two key partners in the group in which I worked, had resigned to join another firm, leaving the department with only the senior partner, Felix Kent, and three associates, including me. Carlin and Marlow took with them a number of clients, including the department's two largest ones, representing nearly half the department's revenues. Kent, the firm's godfather and chair of the department, went into a funk, and understandably so. He had brought both of them into the firm.

The firm went into a spiral of declining morale and solidarity. Partners not in the department wanted the scalps of the departed partners. In particular, members of the firm's executive committee wanted blood, believing that the two who left must have breached their fiduciary obligations to the firm and their other partners.

Earlier that year, in what I later viewed as a cruel reality, I had been told that I would become a partner on January 1, 1986. Achieving that status was the proverbial golden ring of the legal profession. Now I faced more of a sinking anchor than a ring. Amid the turmoil, the firm decided to make me a partner a couple of months early, presumably to help retain clients and stem the bleeding of the firm's revenues.

I took on the task with a vengeance, deciding that the two former partners were tantamount to evil twins who had deceived the firm and stolen its property. While I would later learn that such a view was wrong and extremely naive, it was the attitude I needed at the time to deal with the trauma of the moment. I was successful in retaining a number of key clients and actually getting back a few of the ones the two had taken. The hemorrhaging ended and emotions began to calm.

But there was no stopping the growing desire to sue. Some partners in the firm still wanted blood.

For me, however, the lust for vengeance was gone, particularly when I came to realize that neither Marlow nor Carlin had done anything wrong. In fact, they had legitimate beefs with the firm, and they simply decided to leave. That was certainly nothing new in the legal profession.

All I wanted to do was hold on to the clients we had, get some more of them back, and develop new ones. The constant focus on revenge and what the firm should do about them was divisive and diverted the firm's attention away from what really mattered: the firm's future.

Without any authority to do so, I met with Marlow and Carlin and worked out a settlement that was reasonable for everyone. When I presented it to the firm, I was fearful that I'd be fired, new partner or not. Much to my surprise, the firm accepted the settlement and the feud ended.

My "reward" for showing leadership in a time of crisis was to be made a member of the vaunted executive committee. Imagine having just been made a partner and suddenly finding yourself in the top management of a firm where every other partner was at least five years older, many a generation older. It was a very heady moment and one I admit was most pleasant when it happened. And while I certainly had neither sought nor asked for the promotion, I was not about to turn it down. Not only did it mean more money, but it meant a leadership role in the department that I had not previously enjoyed.

Kent and I worked well together. While his "I" philosophy—i.e., rarely thinking in terms of "we"—took some getting used to, it was never so demeaning that it bothered me. And besides, he was very much my senior and deserving of the respect. When he did relegate me to a minor and sometimes embarrassing role in meetings with clients, I brushed it off as old habits that were hard to break. On occasion, I even remarked to him how it sometimes upset me to be treated as if I weren't even in the room. He'd listen, say he understood, and then do the same thing a day or two later. But that was OK. He was a mentor and was clearly giving me more leeway and freedom than he'd given to Marlow and especially to Carlin. I was doing just fine, developing business and learning about operating a collection of partners with inflated egos and selfish interests. No surprise. That's the DNA of lawyers. But as the saying goes, if you are not the lead dog, the view never changes or, more bluntly, only the lead dog isn't licking the balls of the rest of the pack. I preferred not to be a ball licker.

My management role in the firm also grew, but not without some tense moments.

When the recession of the early '90s hit, things got tough. Law firms across the country closed their doors and went bankrupt. Banks tightened the squeeze on the remaining firms' credit lines, and accounts receivable aging grew by leaps and bounds, cutting off cash flow. More lawyers were unemployed than ever before. It was ugly. While the firm was hardly immune to the pressures, it had never engaged in aggressive debt leveraging, so there was breathing room. But there was also growing discontent among younger partners tired of seeing profits going to senior underperformers.

I recruited key partners on the executive committee to support what amounted to a bloodbath of cuts, including nearly a third of the partners, executed in two phases.

When it came to confronting the partners we were cutting, no one else on the executive committee wanted to be the Grim Reaper. The task fell to me. Others on the committee just didn't have the stomach for the dirty work. It gives me no pride that I was the executioner, but it had to be done. In the end, we nearly halved the size of the firm and began a series of successful years of profit growth. We also added more attorneys along the way and by 1998, we were nearly as large as we had been prior to the first reorganization.

Eventually, the executive committee evolved into two people, Sam Friedman and me. Friedman was a generous and compassionate man. He had a sense of the big picture quite unlike anyone I've known, and could stabilize even the most precarious of moments. Friedman's only problem was that he was terrible at delivering bad news or discipline to anyone.

Unexpectedly, Friedman died. His passing was a great personal loss for me. He was an anchor of reason amid stormy seas. He helped keep me focused on the tasks involved in running a firm and balancing the egos of dozens of lawyers. When he died, the firm decided not to replace him and I became the sole executive partner, operating in a fashion similar to a chairman and CEO. I had the last say in all matters.

Under my individual leadership, the firm continued to grow. Profits increased every year.

The burden of being a single executive partner, however, took a toll. In addition, without Friedman as a comrade in arms, some of the decisions I made did not sit well with those who were affected, particularly when I did not compensate them at levels they felt appropriate to their contributions.

In 2001, a few of my partners approached me and suggested we again add a second executive partner. Their stated reason was to lessen my personal burden and to address the time I was away, which was admittedly often. Absentee leadership in any organization is difficult. They felt a second executive partner who was more likely to be in the office daily would be a better situation. I agreed, and Peter Raymond, the chair of the litigation department, became the second executive partner.

New Yorkers are known for their attitude. Known for being arrogant and impolite. It's a reputation that is largely wrong but does drive New Yorkers to keep the myth going. We like it. After all, New York City is the center of the universe, a conclusion that is widely shared by those who work within its canyons, from Wall Street to Park Avenue.

I was no different when I ran a law firm, and by the late 1980s I had decided it was time to export our dominance to other cities in need of our superiority. At least that's what I told myself.

Hollywood has a lure for everyone, including callous New Yorkers. I had always wanted to have an office on the West Coast, and when in 1989 a firm named Gollenbach & Burrell was splitting up, their Century City office in Los Angeles was in play. I convinced my partners that we needed to make a play. Within a couple of months we welcomed three partners and two of their associates to the firm.

I decided I'd move to Los Angeles for the summer of 1989 to oversee the transition, getting to know my new partners and clients.

I rented a house in Brentwood and a car from Hertz.

I learned quickly the importance of your car in Los Angeles. First, it was the only way to get around. It seemed no one took buses or taxis, and there was no subway. Quite the contrast to New York. And wherever you went, they seemed to have valet parking that cost an arm and a leg. I thought that was quaint. I was used to paying arms and legs for parking in New York. In Los Angeles, parking extortion was at least polite, with valet service. Last, you were definitely judged by the car you drove. My rental, for example, put me in the lower tier of the hoi polloi. But the folks who had Mercedes, Porsches, and Jags were the landed gentry. And if you were driving a Rolls or Bentley, you were royalty. Cars were often ornaments at hotels and restaurants as well. Those driven by royalty and some of the nicer ones driven by the landed gentry were always neatly lined up in front of the hotel or restaurant. The message was clear: *Important people come here. So be impressed.* I made a mental note that if I ever moved to Los Angeles, I'd have to get rid of my mundane Lexus and seriously trade up.

I then met the first client.

At the end of the meeting, he asked, "Do you validate?"

I had no idea what he was talking about.

"Do I validate? If you mean do I believe what you've told me, yes. Is that what you're asking?"

Looking at me as if I were an idiot, he responded, "No. I want to know if you validate parking. Here's my parking ticket."

This guy has got to be kidding, I thought. He wants us to pay for his parking? Doesn't he understand clients pay us, not vice versa?

We went to the receptionist and I asked if we validated. She knew what it meant.

"Yes, of course." She took out a book of coupons that looked like something you'd buy at the post office.

"How many hours do you need?"

The client responded, "How about four so I can do some shopping while I'm here?" With that, the receptionist peeled off four coupons and attached them to the parking ticket. The client bid us farewell, free parking in hand.

"Do we always validate parking?"

"If the client asks, yes."

"And do we always give them extra hours so they can go shopping?"

"Yes. The mall is just around the corner and clients like to shop there or get a meal."

Later that day I bumped into my partner, Fred Ansis. Fred is a celebrated music lawyer and a genuinely unique character.

"Fred," I asked, "What's with paying for clients' parking? We sure don't do that in New York."

"Really? It's normal here. Just like the firm pays for my parking."

Damn, I thought, the firm pays for Fred's parking. They don't pay for mine!

I concluded that Los Angeles was the land of cars and comps. It was all about what you drove and what you got other people to pay for. I liked it.

We eventually moved the offices to Beverly Hills and our practice grew. While we gained and lost some partners and associates, we were profitable. When I later joined Reed Smith, Fred and another lawyer from the Beverly Hills office, Steve Sessa, joined me. And they're both still with Reed Smith.

In 2001, I turned my sights to Chicago, the Windy City. I convinced myself and my partners that we'd do great in Chicago, just as we did in Beverly Hills. We recruited lawyers, rented space, and launched a great marketing campaign with the slogan, "Hall Dickler. When No Is Not the Answer You Need." I thought it was brilliant.

It didn't help that we opened the office just a couple of weeks before the terrorist attacks occurred on September 11, 2001. The Chicago market, along with most of the country, fell into a malaise. Our office never recovered, and its life as part of Hall Dickler was short. We closed it within another year. The only wind we had brought to Chicago was hot air.

The turn for the worse began in mid-2002, when finances were stretched and another reorganization was needed. We agreed to fire some people and demote others from partner to counsel status. Everyone recognized that doing so would mean 2002 would be an "investment year." Nonetheless, we all decided that the changes would be in the best interest of the firm long-term. We also added three more partners to the executive committee.

When it came time to implement the changes, however, it was like déjà vu: most everyone scattered to the hills to avoid being the one delivering bad news. That role fell primarily on the executive partners' shoulders.

Things progressed slowly as we watched the financial performance. In the end, 2002 proved to be a lot worse than just an "investment year." The year end was looking terrible in comparison to other years. The tragedy of 9/11 had taken its toll on our business. Our receivables grew and our cash dissipated. It became obvious that we were going to end the year in the red, drawing out more cash as partners than the firm made in profits.

We took steps to right the ship and 2003 started to look better, but not good enough. It was time to explore options. The best alternative was to pursue a merger with another firm. We started down that path but were eventually thrown off track late in 2003 when a key partner took ten lawyers and left for another firm.

It was time to move on with what we had left, so we dove into looking for a merger partner. When I retained a headhunter for the project, I told her at the outset that I didn't want a firm "born" in New York or Los Angeles because I knew they'd be assholes. She found me three, one from Washington, D.C., another from Atlanta, and Reed Smith from Pittsburgh. In the end, the Washington and Atlanta firms tried to cherry pick from our group, something they were specifically warned against doing. So I guess there are assholes in those cities, too. But Reed Smith played no such games and made offers to twenty-two attorneys and more than a dozen supporting staff. In February 2004, I became an equity partner in Reed Smith, bringing with me more than thirty people from Hall Dickler.

Reed Smith gave me extensive leeway to grow the business. Many of my new partners understood the nature of partnership and were always ready to share and work together. While some were reluctant at first to expose me and my group to their clients, as we succeeded in pitches one after the other, doubters faded away and more and more opened doors. The practice grew. And it's been a wild and successful ride ever since.

chapter 14
Fire Him

Early in my legal career at Hall Dickler, there was one client I really wanted to get: The Association of National Advertisers. The trade association's membership was virtually every global brand—the movers and shakers who had their finger on the pulse in business and politics.

I mapped out a plan.

Two people were key to my pursuing the opportunity. John Sarsen was the association's president and CEO. Gil Weil was their general counsel. I resolved to get to know them both.

I thought it was a pretty smart plan. Weil had been working with the ANA since 1935 and was, I assumed, close to retirement. I reasoned that the association had no one in the wings to replace him, so if I got close enough to him and Sarsen, I'd have a good chance of becoming the next ANA general counsel.

I realized I would never replace Weil as long as he held the position. He'd been with the ANA longer than anyone and was a legend in the business. No one in their right mind could harbor the illusion they could replace him, although that's admittedly contrary to the way most lawyers think. Their egos generally believe they're better than anyone else and can replace anyone with better results. Of course that's preposterous, but so is a lot more about the way lawyers think.

Knowing Weil was entrenched, I decided to volunteer to help him as he saw fit. And I made sure Sarsen was aware of my "pro bono" contributions.

This went on for years and I got close to Weil. He relied on me more and more for some work, and Sarsen grew to appreciate what I was doing.

This all required a great deal of patience. More than I ever thought would be needed.

After providing free services for more than ten years, I thought Weil would never retire. And while I'd gotten Sarsen to the point where he promised me the position once Gil retired, I was beginning to think Weil would be the longest-living lawyer in human history. But he was a wonderful man and I wished him health. I just wanted him to retire.

Tragically, Weil died on April 22, 2002. The story has it that he died while typing minutes of the latest ANA board meeting. That does not surprise me. Weil was one of those lawyers who loved what he did, and I'd come to realize he would never retire alive. The difference with Weil, unlike other lawyers who overstay their welcome, was that he was sharp right to the end. He never missed a beat. Years after his death, some folks pushed for him to be inducted into the American Advertising Federation's Hall of Fame. Despite glowing recommendations, including one from me, the AAF passed and Weil has never been given the honor. Shame on the AAF.

Shortly after Weil passed away, Sarsen called me and true to his word offered me the job.

"There's just one problem, Doug," he said in conclusion.

"What's that, John?"

"We have no money and can't pay you."

I knew Weil was being paid something, and *Advertising*

Age reported that Sarsen was paid over $600,000 in 2001. How could there be no money?

I was shocked. I'd worked for free for more than ten years providing thousands of dollars of free legal advice and my payoff was now to be zero in fees?

But I'd worked for this jewel so long that I couldn't imagine walking away. I had too much equity in the game.

"John, are you sure I can't at least get a nominal retainer? I really need some fees to justify to my partners."

"I'll see what I can do, but I need to know if you want the job. There's work that needs to be done and I need to find someone to do it."

Find some other sucker who didn't pay his dues and give him or her the prize? There was no way I was going to let that happen.

"OK, John. As long as I have your assurance we'll see what we can do in the future, I'm honored to become the ANA's General Counsel."

And who said lawyers are never whores. We often are.

A lot of work needed to be done. I learned quickly that Weil had a number of projects under way that needed attention, and the ANA's annual meeting was fast approaching. Their annual meeting was a major industry event that attracted major players. Or at least I assumed it did.

When October 2002 came, I found myself in Florida for my first annual meeting as general counsel to the ANA. While I had to pay my own way, that didn't diminish the excitement I felt. It took a long time to get this ring and I was going to get as much out of it as I could. Particularly since I wasn't being paid.

In the tradition of the ANA, the day before the full conference begins, the ANA board of directors holds a meeting. I wasn't sure if I was supposed to attend or not but volunteered to do so. They were supposed to start the meeting at 2:00 p.m.

I got a call at about 12:30 from one of the board members I knew.

"Doug, can you come down to the conference room? We're in the board meeting and we have a question for you."

"Of course." That was exciting. They actually were reaching out to me. The top chief marketing officers in the world were reaching out to me. I was convinced I'd finally begin to get the payoff for all the years of free work.

After being introduced to the board, the chairman asked me a question.

"Doug, who do you work for? The board or John Sarsen?"

The answer was easy. "I work for the ANA at the pleasure of both the board and John."

"But do you ultimately answer to the board or Sarsen?"

"The board," I answered.

"Good," responded the chairman. "We want you to fire him."

Fire him? The guy who just hired me? Were they kidding?

But I had my orders and I carried them out. I won't even speculate how Sarsen, who died in 2011, felt about me or lawyers in general.

After doing as instructed, I was introduced to Bob Liodice, an ANA staffer who the board appointed as "interim president."

The challenge Liodice faced was daunting. The first thing was the reality that the ANA actually didn't have any money. Sarsen wasn't kidding me. Liodice had become the captain of what might well have been the *Titanic* of trade associations.

But Liodice was a financial guy. He dove into the challenge and over the years turned the ANA into the biggest and most influential advertising trade association in the world. Today, the ANA is the Big Kahuna.

Luckily, Liodice didn't fire me and I remain the general counsel of the ANA to this day. And I'm being paid.

chapter 15
My Friend Newt

When George W. Bush was president, I was a bit of a political junkie, more aligned with the Republicans than the Democrats. In hindsight I'm not entirely sure why, but they seemed more in tune with my moderate point of view than the predominantly liberal Democrats. So I donated a few hundred dollars to the Republican National Committee.

Talk about pit bulls! Once they identified me as a potential donor, the solicitations for more and more just kept coming. It got to the point where it was overwhelming, so I just started throwing the letters away. I'd decided my donations really didn't have any impact and I was growing disgusted with the waste in government.

After ignoring the Republicans for about a year, in 2002 I got a letter congratulating me on being chosen to receive a gold medal as a great supporter of their cause. I was invited to come to Washington to receive my much-deserved award from none other than Newt Gingrich, the Speaker of the House of Representatives.

My first inclination was to throw the invite into the same trash can where I'd thrown all the other requests. But my assistant, Nancy Schulein, insisted I go. She said it would be fun and that I should take my good friend, Mitch Becker, with me and have a good time in Washington.

I called Mitch and asked him if he'd like to go. I promised I'd get a limo to tool around in and we'd have some fun. Mitch, never one to pass up a good time, quickly agreed.

We rendezvoused in the capital, limo ready, and went to the hotel where I was to receive my gold medal. What we encountered was sad.

Literally hundreds of people were there, all of whom were receiving the coveted award. They were just everyday folks, all of whom had been snookered into giving the Republicans their hard-earned money and thinking this was a crowning moment for their patriotism and love of country.

We all lined up for our moment with Speaker Gingrich. When it came to my turn, Mitch and I stood on either side of him for the official photo and I was given the medal. It took about a minute after standing in the line for almost an hour. I don't remember what he said to us. It doesn't matter. What bothered me was not that I'd wasted my money but that so many others had done the same under the illusion that it made a difference. It doesn't.

Mitch and I went off in our limo to the various monuments in Washington: the Lincoln Memorial, Jefferson Memorial, Washington Monument, and more. We hit most of them and took pictures of one another wearing the medal. We were like kids in a candy store.

When people noticed and asked what we were doing or who we were, Mitch told them I was a VIP who just got the gold medal from Newt Gingrich for my great service to America. Some asked to have a picture with me. We obliged.

At the Jefferson Memorial, two kids came up with a video camera, telling us they were from George Washington University and were doing a school documentary on capital happenings. When Mitch gave them the story, they asked if I would allow them to interview me on camera for their film. Of course, I consented and opined on all things political. Total BS. But they seemed to like it. To this day, I wonder where that video is and whether it ever made it into their documentary. I wonder if they actually thought they were interviewing someone important or influential, which I wasn't.

As I look back upon that day, it truly saddens me how our political process misleads people who have so many hopes in a better future that they are willing to give donations to political parties that really don't care about them for causes the politicians will forget as soon as the money is in their hands.

Today, I don't give money to either party or any politician. They don't deserve it. No doubt if any of them worked for me in the private sector, I would have fired them.

My attitude is admittedly cynical. But that's true of so many today. The little guy's money doesn't move Washington's agenda one iota. It's the big donations and lobbyists that influence legislation. More often than not, the everyday voter gets nothing.

But at least I have a gold medal.

chapter 16
Is Daddy a Nazi?

The First Amendment to our Constitution guarantees, among other things, our freedom of speech. It is unique in the world. No other country has the concept established as an inalienable right. Lawyers have a passion for it—sometimes to a point at which any logical person would wonder about their sanity. How many times have you heard intelligent people bitch about causes taken up by the American Civil Liberties Union defending the rights of some of the most reprehensible people on earth? A good lawyer will tell you that while such emotional responses are understandable, they cannot be allowed to trump First Amendment rights.

Here's an example of my zealot defense of the First Amendment and how I failed to convince my then seven-year-old daughter of the wisdom behind it. She's now a lawyer herself and, as far as I know, understands what I tried to teach her many years ago.

In the late '90s I was invited to appear on Court TV, a cable station that thankfully had very few viewers, to debate the First Amendment rights of tobacco companies. The show was produced in St. Paul, Minnesota, in a beautiful landmark building. I was given the side of the debate defending Big Tobacco. On the opposite side of the debate was Hubert Humphrey Jr., the son of the former vice president of the United States. I should have bowed out right then and there, but my ego would not let me.

I decided to take my son, Joshua, and daughter, Meghan, with me so they could see how a live television show was produced. I knew they'd love Minneapolis with its skyways that allow you to walk all over the city without ever going outside. And I planned to take them to the Mall of America too. It was going to be a father/son/daughter outing. A happy time.

When I arrived, I was introduced to the other two people on my "panel." One was the head of the Minnesota Tobacco Coalition and the other someone, the one I best recall, reminded me of an ex-con who looked as if he'd been smoking about ten cartons a day. The other two members of Humphrey's panel were a police officer and a physician, both of whom looked straight out of central casting. Officer Bolton and Dr. Kildare.

To top it off, the "audience" was divided in two as well. On Humphrey's side there were about fifty or so kids who looked like they were all honor society members. On my side, there were about fifty juvenile delinquents with more tattoos than the Navy.

It was a complete setup. But my kids were there and I could not let them down. I resolved to rise to the occasion and try to explain that while I didn't defend smoking, I believed that the First Amendment guaranteed anyone—even Big Tobacco—to speak what was true, and absent proof that they were making false or deceptive claims, they had a right to advertise.

Let's just say it didn't go very well.

When it mercifully concluded, and I was sufficiently bloodied by Humphrey and the moderator (and by some snotty teenager as well), I collected Meghan and Josh and began the walk to the hotel.

Unsure what to say, I asked the two of them what they thought.

Meghan responded, "Daddy, I'm never talking to you again."

Crushed, I asked, "Why?"

"Because you're saying it's OK to smoke and it's not OK to smoke."

I wasn't sure whether I should feel bad that she didn't understand the First Amendment and the difference between behavior and speech or feel happy that she thought smoking was a bad thing.

We went on to the hotel (silently) and got ready for dinner.

At dinner, I decided I could not let my daughter think I was condoning smoking—which I was not—or bear the thought that she'd never talk to me again.

I asked her, "Meghan, at the TV show today, did you understand what I was trying to say about the First Amendment?"

She looked confused.

I continued, "I do not think it's a good thing to smoke. I think it's a terrible thing to do. And I don't want you to ever do it."

She still looked confused.

I went on, "The First Amendment isn't about protecting only good things people say. Or only protecting what you like to hear people say. It's about allowing people to say things even if we disagree. It protects open conversations where we learn from one another." Or some other claptrap along those lines.

Obviously, she still looked confused and Josh was simply shaking his head, getting more interested in his hamburger than the conversation.

So I decided to simplify it so even a seven-year-old could understand. After all, I am a lawyer and certainly know how to make even complicated principles seem simple.

"Meghan, do you know what a Nazi is?"

"I think so."

"A Nazi is a terrible person. Their ideas are bad. No one likes them. But the only way we know how stupid they are is if we let them say all the idiotic things they believe. So by defending their right to speak, we learn how awful they are. If we never let them speak, we'd never learn to reject what they say. Do you understand that?"

She looked at me and asked, "Daddy, are you a Nazi?"

Josh said, "Dad, give it up. You can't explain it."

I ordered another scotch.

chapter 17
Respecting the Chicago Cubs

In 1994 when my son, Josh, was in seventh grade, he told me he wanted me to coach a recreational league baseball team—the Wyckoff, New Jersey, version of the Little League. When I asked him why, he told me it was because he wanted to be a pitcher and he didn't think the other coaches would make him one. He'd already played one year and didn't get to pitch. I reminded him that I didn't have a clue how to coach baseball. I never played it as a kid and really didn't follow it much despite claiming to be a Mets fan. But there was no way I could say no.

I signed up and got notified that there would be a draft on a Saturday in April. A *draft*, I thought. For recreational base-ball?

I got a list from Josh of the kids he wanted on the team. I never bothered to ask him if any of them knew the game or were good at it. I didn't ask what positions they played. They were his friends. That's all that mattered to him and me.

When I showed up at the draft, it quickly became clear to me that some of the fathers coaching took it very seriously, as if they were drafting for a professional team. All the kids had been rated from 1 to 3 on ability, with 3 being the highest rating. Each round required that a coach not exceed a certain total when adding up the ratings of the kids. In theory, that forced coaches to have balanced teams. In reality, the coaches in the draft, except for me—the only rookie in the room—were the ones who rated the kids from the previous year. One coach later told me to watch out for the ratings. Some were rigged, with players intentionally rated low so they could get them on teams under the cap. Such bullshit.

When the draft was done, I had the lowest-rated kids in the league. I didn't come close to the cap. The other coaches got a real kick out of it. A stupid rookie. That pissed me off but I realized that I was not in a position to play the game they played. I took my team back to Josh. He was thrilled. It was full of his friends, most of whom couldn't hit the side of a barn judging from the ratings they received.

The town assigned a team name. I got the Cubs. Mind you not the official Chicago Cubs. Just the Cubs with crummy uniforms and cheap hats.

Our first practice was a disaster. Not only did I not know the game well enough to coach it intelligently, I had a team of total misfits. We should have been the "Bad News Bears." My stroke of luck was two assistant coaches—fathers of kids on the team—who knew the game inside out. They would prove to be my saving grace.

Over the next two weeks, I read everything I could find on coaching kids in baseball. I consulted with my friend, Mark Steinberger, one of the Boys of the RCH, on what to do. He was a bona fide athlete who played baseball and later became a Small College All American in football. He urged me to find ways to motivate the kids to have fun and swing at every pitch. "Just get the ball in play," he said.

At the end of the third practice, I assembled the team. Some parents were there. I did four things. First, I gave each of the kids two brand-new baseballs. I told them that if they were going to play for me, I expected them to have a new set of balls. They laughed. I'm not sure how the parents felt. Second, I told them I would not play the game the way I'd been told other coaches did. The league had a rule that kids had to play a minimum of innings in each game. While that seemed fair, it was not. The rule was not that they all had to play the same number; therefore, a coach could bench marginal players. And if they played the less-talented kids late in the game, those kids might not play at all if the game was called for time. That meant that some kids only got to play two or three innings. I told the team that everyone would play the same number of innings regardless of ability. To back that up, I told them I'd post the roster before every game. Third, I told them they'd all get to play every position they wanted to play at some point in the season. The only exception was pitching. To be a pitcher, they had to show me their stuff first. I didn't want any of them to be embarrassed on the mound. And finally, I unveiled new hats. I bought genuine Chicago Cubs hats to replace the crappy hats the town supplied.

The kids went nuts. They loved it all. We were off and running.

We played games on Saturdays, Tuesdays, and Thursdays. By the third game, we were 2-1. We weren't supposed to be. We were supposed to be the team that everyone beat.

As I stood by the bench during the fourth game, a representative from the Recreation Department handed me an envelope, telling me I should read the notice. The letter inside read that my hats were illegal and the kids would have to stop wearing the official Chicago Cubs hats, replacing them with the crappy hats the town provided. I was shocked.

After we won the game that Tuesday night and were 3-1,

I told the kids we'd have to ditch the hats. Rules were rules. I was later told the name of the coach who complained to the Rec Department about the hats. I couldn't believe a father would be so incensed that he'd lost to my team that he'd make an issue out of frickin' hats. What a jerk, I remember thinking.

The kids reacted badly, lamenting that they'd now suck. They said they couldn't win without the hats. I told them that was silly. We were 3-1 and there was no reason we couldn't win again without the hats.

On Thursday, we lost. Big time. We were slaughtered 7 to nothing. As the end of the game, the kids all said it was because of the hats. As far as they were concerned, the team sucked without them.

On Friday, on my way into the office, I tried to think of ways to regain their enthusiasm and confidence. Then it hit me. I'd buy a bunch of Chicago Cubs hat pins and every time they made a good play, I'd give them a pin for their crappy hats. I was inspired by the helmet decals Ohio State gave their football players on good plays.

I called Modell's, a local sporting goods store, from my cell phone.

"We don't have Cubs hat pins," I was told. "We only have the Yankees and Mets."

"So where can I get Chicago Cubs pins?" I asked.

The store clerk responded, "I don't know. I guess you can get them in Chicago."

With the next game only a day away, I was faced with a dilemma. Do I buy Mets or Yankee pins? That didn't make sense. We were the Cubs. Other teams were the Mets and Yankees.

So instead of going to the office, I drove to LaGuardia airport and flew to Chicago. I bought every Chicago Cubs hat pin

I could find in the airport stores. And I bought Cubs foam rubber fingers, women's earrings, and Cubs banners for the fans. I got on a flight back to New York with two bags filled with Cubs stuff.

On the plane, I stuffed the bags under the seat in front of me. The guy beside me asked, "Gee, are you a real Cubs fan or what?"

I told him no and related the story to him, telling him I was actually a Mets fan. He asked for my name and the town where I coached. I happily told him as the two of us enjoyed some cocktails.

On Saturday, I passed out the Cubs stuff and announced the pin policy. We ended the game in a tie.

The next day, I got an email from a friend in Chicago. It seems that the guy I was sitting beside was a reporter for the *Chicago Tribune*. The paper ran a tongue-in-cheek article about how the Mets were once again trying to deny the Cubs a championship. It was hilarious. And it was picked up by the AP. On Monday, it appeared in the local paper. Then everything hit the fan.

On Tuesday, I was told my pins could not be put on the hats. Once again, the Rec Department issued an edict without any warning. Now I was pissed.

On Wednesday, I filed a notice of claim against the town for violating New Jersey's Sunshine Act, which prohibited towns from having meetings without public notice so those affected had a chance to participate. I told the team that while we'd have to follow the order, we weren't done yet. I refused to let them feel taken advantage of by a jealous coach and manipulated Rec Department. Talk about being an asshole attorney! I had thirty days to file suit.

What ensued over the next few weeks was spellbinding.

The local paper showed up at the next game and asked that we line up our hats along the first-base line for a photo. The team happily did so. The article quoted a local politician supporting my position. He later recanted. No doubt pressured to do so. In town, I got high fives from most people, although a few thought I was a complete jerk. I didn't care. The kids on my team needed to have their say and a lesson in civics and due process. What the town did may have been right by the rules of the game, but it was wrong in the way they did it.

As we won and lost a few more games, the day of reckoning came when I had to either file suit or shut up. To be honest, I was in a panic. I had never filed such a suit and was a bit in the dark about how best to frame it. I resolved to explain it as best I could to the kids that I would not be filing suit.

A week before the deadline, I got a call from the town attorney.

"Doug, what do you want? You can't be serious about suing the town."

"I am serious," I bluffed. "But if you want me to back down, I'll do so if I get a letter of apology from the mayor to the kids for denying them the opportunity to have their say before the edicts from the Rec Department were delivered. If you get me that letter together with a promise that I will not be blackballed from coaching in the future, I will drop the threat to sue."

"I don't think that's possible," he responded.

"Then I guess I'll see you in court," I said in my best asshole attorney tone. We ended the call and I damn near panicked. Now what do I do?

I started looking for forms and articles on suing under the Sunshine Act. I was running out of time.

Then my wife called and read me a letter that had been hand-delivered to the house. It was from the mayor expressing his regrets that the kids didn't get the chance to participate in the decision to ban the hats. It was as close to an apology as I could expect. Even local officials are politicians focused on spin.

I felt both relieved and gratified. It was a great lesson for the kids. Never back down when your rights to participate in a decision are denied. Maybe to some I was acting like an asshole attorney, but it felt right.

We finished the season 6-3-1 and went on to lose in the first game of the playoffs, largely because I followed my rule of everyone playing. And while the kids were disappointed by the loss, they were as proud as any team of misfits could be. They might not have won the championship, but they were champions.

I coached for two more seasons, until my son went into high school. We never did win a championship, but I was voted coach of the year in 1996. And while I was told a couple of parents asked the Recreation Department not to have me draft their kid, it never came up when we picked the teams. In truth, many parents asked the opposite. They knew that if I coached, their kids played.

I made sure we had fun every season. On a lark, in the season that followed the pro baseball strike, I asked the Mets to send a player to one of our games as a gesture of goodwill to the kids who were disappointed during the strike. Much to my surprise, they sent Tim Bogar, a utility player and great guy. He took the kids to a local batting cage and taught them how a big-leaguer hits. In another year, as a gift to my assistant coaches, I took a long shot and wrote to Hillary Clinton, Warren Buffett, and Ringo Starr with a request that they sign an enclosed baseball. One was for a female coach who admired Clinton, one was for a coach who worked as a stockbroker, and the final one was for the coach who loved the drums. Amazingly, Starr and Buffett both returned signed balls. Buffet even sent me a personal letter and a second ball he signed from the Omaha Royals, his team. And while Clinton declined, the White House had then vice president Al Gore sign the ball. That was good enough for me. Through the seasons, we had caricature artists, hot-dog vendors, clowns, and more at games. All I had to do was ask folks to come. Amazing what you get when you ask for it.

What remains my crowning moment was during the second season in a game against the coach who complained about the Cubs hats. All the asshole cared about was winning. And as they say, "revenge is a dish best served cold."

In the third or fourth inning, the bases were loaded and there was one out. I gave Tommy Barrett, my best bunter, the sign for a suicide squeeze—a play where the runner on third base leaves third for the plate as the pitcher delivers the ball, hopefully reaching home before the catcher can retrieve the ball to tag him out. But doing it with bases loaded is an insane call by any baseball standards. All the catcher has to do is pick up the ball, step on the plate, and the runner from third is out. Then a simple throw to first base makes the third out and the inning is over. But we were there to have some fun, and I'd done trick plays successfully all season.

Tommy took the sign and stepped back from the batter's box looking confused. I gave the sign again. And it wasn't as though my signs were difficult to understand. The sign for a suicide squeeze was making a choking sign on my neck with my hand. Nothing could have been clearer—for everyone, including the opposing team. But Tommy was still confused.

So I called time and walked to the plate to talk to him. I asked, "Tommy, did you see the sign?"

"Yes, coach, but I don't understand."

"Tommy, just go with it. Let's have some fun."

As I passed my team's bench on my way back to the third-base coaching box, I told them to start screaming as soon as we sent the runners on the pitch. "Go nuts," I said.

The pitcher began his windup and I sent the runners. The bunt was perfect and slowly started to dribble toward the mound. The catcher panicked and rather than going back to tag home, he threw the ball to second base but tossed it over the fielder's head. It bounded into center field. The runners kept advancing. Two runs in. The center fielder reached the ball and tried for an out at the plate. Three runs in. At this point, Tommy was already rounding third base. The ball went over the catcher's head and hit the backstop. Tommy scored. A grand slam suicide squeeze. Our team and fans went crazy. We went on to win.

The other coach was apoplectic, screaming at his team using very colorful epithets describing their abilities as ball players. I thought he was going to have a heart attack. I only regret I didn't have a Cubs hat with me. It would have been sweet to put it on.

chapter 18
Daddy Is a Dweeb

When my daughter, Meghan, was thirteen she announced at dinner that she had a boyfriend. My interrogation skills immediately kicked in.

"When do I get to meet your boyfriend?" I asked.

"Why do you want to meet him?" asked Meghan.

"Because that's what fathers always do. They meet their daughter's boyfriends."

"I never heard of that."

"Well, now you have."

Not exactly one of those precious father/daughter moments.

We went on to whatever the next topic was and finished our meal.

The next weekend, I was out on errands in my British racing green BMW Z3, beige top down, leather seats gleaming. As I pulled into my driveway, at the end of the macadam stood Meghan and her new boyfriend, who looked like a slob. I immediately concluded I didn't like him, not really giving a damn about the facts.

Meghan said, "Hi, Daddy. This is [I can't remember the reprobate's name]."

"Hello, Mr. Wood," said the reprobate.

I couldn't help but notice how he was admiring my car.

"Cool car," he said.

For reasons I'll never understand, I responded, "Yes, it is. Would you like to go for a ride?"

"Sure."

I looked at Meghan, "Meghan, there's only two seats in the car so you're on your own for a few minutes." I motioned for the reprobate to get in the car.

Off we drove with me trying to drive as if I were James Bond, shifting more than I needed to so the roar of the engine would impress the testosterone-strewn teenager in the passenger seat.

"So you like my daughter, huh?"

"Yeah."

Yeah? How about "Yes, sir?" But I let it pass.

"OK. Well, I have three rules." Much like I can't remember why I ever offered the kid a ride, I have no idea why I said there were three rules. Why not two or four? I'll never know.

"OK," he responded. A real talker, this kid!

Undaunted, I proceeded.

"The first rule is no smoking."

"Of course, Mr. Wood. I don't smoke. I am an athlete. I play for Ramapo High."

"Good. The second rule is no drinking or drugs." As soon as I said it, I realized I'd just condensed two rules into one, assuming it was a subconscious reaction over my desire to avoid the third rule.

"Absolutely, Mr. Wood. The school doesn't allow its athletes to drink or do drugs."

We continued in silence.

"Mr. Wood, you said there were three rules. What is the third rule?"

At least he could count.

I didn't know how to put this across to him in a way he'd understand. All I could come up with was, "The third rule is I expect you to respect my daughter. Do you understand what that means?"

I could tell by the look in his eyes that his pathetic brain had no idea what I was talking about.

I drove onto the shoulder and stopped the car. I stared at him and said, "Think about it. Do you think you can understand what I mean by respecting my daughter without my having to go into details?"

His expression suddenly changed with a realization that I was talking about . . . sex.

He remained silent, but I didn't need to hear another word from him. Instead, I said, "I expect you to respect my daughter. Because if you don't, I'll kill you."

I started the car and returned home. Not another word was ever exchanged between me and the reprobate.

A few weeks passed and we were once again enjoying a family dinner.

"I have a new boyfriend," announced Meghan.

"When do I get to meet him?" I asked.

"I'm never letting you meet another one of my boyfriends, Daddy. After the last one, everyone thinks you're crazy."

I smiled, knowing I'd done my job.

chapter 19
Hollywood Hopefuls

Slug. You'll Never Go into the Garden Again.

That was the title of the movie screen treatment my two friends, Arnie Lawner and Steve Harvey, and I wrote in 1985. It was a spoof of horror films and centered on an experiment gone wrong in San Francisco (how original!) that creates a giant slug that wreaks havoc across the United States en route to Massachusetts. The heroes, Nick Cleveland, a down-and-out reporter, and Wanda Simpson, a renowned sex therapist, track the slug in what becomes a rather strange romantic triangle. We had a blast writing it, and when it was optioned for a whopping hundred dollars by Grosso-Jacobson Productions, we were in seventh heaven, convinced we were on our way to Hollywood stardom and millions in royalties. We celebrated our newfound fame and blew the hundred dollars in some cheap bar in New York. Didn't matter. We knew we'd have plenty of money coming in soon.

Not quite. The project died on the vine and Grosso-Jacobson never produced it. And our show-business dreams died with it. Therein lies the lesson on options. Don't believe them.

Undaunted, years later the three of us went on to write the *Trollop Hunters Handbook*. Thankfully, that one was never seen by the public either.

But Arnie and I continued to pursue the deal that would

reap in enough so we could retire young, as in by forty. Our list of deals was endless.

We met with International Fragrances & Flavors and the chief chemist from RC Cola in an attempt to introduce a carbonated gin drink that would be sold in 12-ounce bottles. And we had that idea before Bartles & Jaymes introduced the concept. We even came up with a five-pack carton instead of a six pack. We called it a Metropack. We conducted taste tests and honed the product to what we thought was perfection. But the market wasn't ready, no financing was available, and that idea too died on the vine.

When we read that a Wall Street stock brokerage firm was for sale, Arnie and I walked in and tried to buy it on pure leverage. Didn't work. We were thrown out. But at least we tried.

Do you remember those obnoxious capsules with compressed foam rubber inside that ballooned up into dinosaurs and lions when you dissolved them in water? Arnie and I met with a foam extruder and designed a capsule that when dunked in water melted to reveal various sponge body parts. We called it "Things that Get Big and Wet." We didn't have the capital necessary to launch it.

One summer, we decided to go to a hundred different bars. That's a lot harder than it sounds. We got to about sixty.

The list goes on. It included some great ideas:

- Transgraphics—Advertising billboards on the sides of trucks. 3M helped us with the graphics. We signed up a few trucking companies. But no advertisers were interested. Now you see ads on the sides of trucks all the time.

- Bar Buddy—An industrial-grade margarita machine that we tried to sell to local bars. We didn't realize that blenders were a lot cheaper and bars really didn't care if our machine made a much better frozen concoction. So much for the customer comes first concept.

- Page-O-Matic Self Pager—This nifty device looked like a pager but it was nothing more than a self-setting beeper on a one-minute delay. You secretly press the button and wait until it goes off. Then you tell those you're with that you have an emergency and have to leave. Great way to get out of a social engagement gone bad. Didn't sell.

- War-Torn Area Tours—Prepackaged tours to dangerous areas of the world that were in the middle of wars or insurgent attacks. Pretty sick idea. We dropped it.

- Justifications, Inc.—An organization you call when you're in a jam and need an explanation or excuse. Need a receipt? Call Justifications, Inc. Need an excuse for missing a deadline or meeting? Call Justifications, Inc. In the end, we decided it was too close to fraud.

- Bulk Brothers—The two of us visited restaurants and provided them with a business card that said we were the Bulk Brothers, restaurant critics. We figured we'd get some free meals. Not.

Over the years, we had more than sixty ideas. As I look at the list today, some still baffle me as to what they were: On Hold with Music, Will Depository, Survivalist Camps, Testing for Toxic Waste, Salad Cookies, Iranian Stamps, Toilet & Tub Cleaning Kits, Septic Saver and more.

None of our deals made us a dime with the exception of one: The Immoral Minority. In the late '70s and early '80s, evangelist Jerry Falwell founded the Moral Majority, a conservative religious group opposed to just about everything on the liberal agenda. And while Arnie, Harv, and I were not conservatives or liberals per se, we found the hypocrisy of the Moral Majority fascinating and decided to "fight back" with the Immoral Minority. We created local clubs that paid dues, and we supplied them with buttons and bumper stickers. It was particularly popular on college campuses. We attended rallies holding signs for the Immoral Minority with the slogan "Lust is a Must," taking liberty with Jimmy Carter's admission in *Playboy* magazine that he lusted for some women. We appeared on radio talk shows as the Johnson brothers, never using our real names. We wrote the *Immoral Minority Manifesto* and printed it on parchmentlike paper. We had a blast and made some money, albeit not much more than enough to buy beers, but it was a profit all the same. And today, if you search the Internet for the Immoral Minority, you find some knockoffs. But the original that started it all is gone. Maybe the knockoffs got the idea from us in the '80s before the Internet was born. Or perhaps not. Doesn't matter.

So our batting average was about .014. Not exactly Hall of Fame, but it sure was fun trying to get into the big leagues.

More recently, I've been bouncing around an idea with my friend Mitch Becker. We call it *The Fifty-Pound Lobster*. It's a book about arrogant assholes who think they're untouchable—just like a fifty-pound lobster—until the day they get caught.

Our plan is to trace the phenomenon from Louie XVI and Marie Antoinette through to David Petraeus, Bill O'Reilly, and the rest of the lineup of sexual harassers in the press. All arrogant blowhards that thought their shit didn't stink, until they got caught and fell from grace. Hard. We'll start the book someday after a cocktail or two.

The lessons from all of this are many. First, no one gets your creative juices running better than your friends. Second, have some guts to do things that are absurd. It's a lot of fun. Third, and most important, there is nothing better than dreaming. The fact that most of your dreams will never be fulfilled isn't relevant. Remember, there is only one thing that is certain—none of your dreams will be fulfilled if you don't have any.

chapter 20
9/11 Remembered

Just as our parents all remember where they were on December 7, 1941, when Japan attacked Pearl Harbor, and many of us recall where we were on November 22, 1963, when John F. Kennedy was assassinated, none of us will ever forget where we were on September 11, 2001, when terrorists felled the World Trade Center towers.

I was on the George Washington Bridge sitting in traffic with a direct line of sight to the World Trade Center. I missed seeing the first plane hit by a few minutes but had a front-row seat for the second hit.

A month later, I was asked to write about it by my law school. Here's what I wrote:

> September 11 could not have been a more beautiful day as I approached the George Washington Bridge, the mid-point of my daily commute from New Jersey. There wasn't a cloud in the sky and the air was as clear as I can ever remember.
>
> The humor of the disc jockey on the radio was interrupted with the report that a plane had hit the north tower. As almost everyone else initially thought, I assumed it was a small private plane. As I crossed the bridge and the reports got more serious, I could

see the two towers in the distant sky. As I looked at the towers while traffic proceeded slowly, the second plane hit the south tower. From the bridge, it was impossible to tell which tower was hit. I assume it was the same tower with another explosion. It didn't take long for the radio to report our worst fears.

By the time I arrived at my office (on the corner of Third Avenue and 54th Street—a good distance from Ground Zero), it seemed the entire sky to the south was covered in a black shroud. People were walking around in a daze. No one was talking. The streets were screaming with sirens from fire trucks, police cars, and emergency vehicles. It was as though all hell had broken loose.

We all huddled around the television at the office, watching along with the rest of America as the two towers fell and reports came in on the other planes. By then, the mass exodus from Manhattan had begun. Every street going north on the East side was bumper to bumper. All the streets south were empty except for the now constant sound of sirens heading down to the disaster.

That afternoon, the mayor shut down all the river crossings, so I was stranded in the city, unable to get home that night. After spending the night with a friend in the city, I awoke at 5:00 a.m., unable to sleep and decided to walk the seven or so blocks back to my office. The scene as I walked to my office was something out of a Fellini movie. Barely a soul was on the streets, except for the occasional pairing of police in riot gear on corners. The quiet was only shattered now and again by yet another siren. Otherwise the streets were entirely deserted, occasional pieces of paper meandering their way in the wind down the avenues as if in slow motion. I broke down and cried like a baby as I walked, beginning to realize the gravity of the events.

The crossings to New Jersey were reopened later that morning, so I left at about 10:00 for home, thinking that I'd be stuck in traffic for hours. As I drove up the East River Drive, however, there was barely another car in sight. Southbound, the drive was still closed with military vehicles at every exit, manned with soldiers in full combat gear. The scene became even more unsettling when an F-16, flying at about a thousand or so feet, screamed down the East River, heading south.

That's when it really hit me. This was happening in my home. It was in my front yard. I will never forget that feeling, the anger I had and the fears I felt (particularly as the father of a nineteen-year-old son). None of our lives will ever be the same again.

chapter 21
9/11 Anniversary

One year after 9/11, I was sitting at home most of the day working on my computer with the television on in the background, occasionally looking up to see or hear yet another story about 9/11 and the anniversary of the tragedy. For most of the day, I pretty much ignored the tear jerkers, emotional reporters, and horrific pictures repeated over and over again. Pictures I'd seen all too many times.

Then I got to thinking about what the anniversary was really all about; maybe what every day is all about. I wrote this to my kids:

> While we should never forget what happened on 9/11, we cannot stop celebrating life, knowing that there will always be heroes in times of strife, healers in time of pain, and friends in times of need. Friends that might not have been friends just seconds before, but who become lifelong friends in the flash of an instant. And while there's a lot we'll never understand and too much we can't forgive that others do, we can't lose sight of all the good so many people do, day in and day out.
>
> A reporter for the *New York Times* once lamented that our pop culture has gone too far and minimized

the world around us with trite songs by Britney Spears, hucksterism by one seller after another, sports heroes pumped up on steroids, and a preoccupation with ourselves, rather than the "bigger picture." But the reporter was dead wrong. The pop culture we live with today is simply a reflection of what we do to relax in a world that is all too easily overwhelming. Indeed, I can't even imagine the stress and pressures our political leaders suffer in these times. What they know but don't tell us for our own good. What they do silently to protect us all. We should be grateful for pop culture and its diversion.

So what's this little lament by me mean? What message do I want it to leave with you?

It's pretty simple. Whatever happens in the world or whatever happens in our lives, no matter how personally upsetting they may be, we need to remember that it's going to be OK. The bad things will pass with time. We'll always heal. And we'll heal each other if we let ourselves.

We've all got a choice. We can be a people, and individuals who when knocked down, pick ourselves up, dust ourselves off, and look to a bright day ahead every day. Or, we can choose to never see beyond our personal challenges, accepting them in defeat. Personally, I don't think any of us are accepting of defeat. So here's a toast to tomorrow. Another bright day to live life to its fullest.

Nothing less will do.

chapter 22
Potato Chips and the Art of Negotiation

As the 1984 Olympics converged on Los Angeles, I got a call from my client, a now defunct potato chip maker.

"Doug, we're signing Tony Randall and Jack Klugman from the *Odd Couple* TV series as our spokespersons. You need to go to Los Angeles right away and finish the deal."

"Los Angeles?" I responded, "Are you kidding? I'll never get a reservation at any hotel. The Olympics are starting."

"I'll see what I can do."

A few hours later, the client called back.

"We got you a room. Their agent, Abby Greshler, pulled some strings and you have a reservation at the Beverly Hills Hotel. Tomorrow night. One night. You're to meet Greshler in the Palm Court for breakfast to put the deal to bed."

So off to LA I went. The Beverly Hills Hotel no less. Hotel to the stars. Hollywood.

I checked in about 7:00 after a six-hour flight from New York.

"Mr. Wood, we have you in a lovely room overlooking the gardens. I see you're only staying with us one night. Would you like us to arrange for a car to pick you up tomorrow and return you to the airport?"

"Yes. That would be nice."

The room was wonderful, and I immediately noticed that the bathroom didn't have those little tiny bottles of shampoo. It had full-size bottles! And nice fluffy towels. And a great bathrobe. I immediately knew why the room cost what it did!

Within a half hour, the doorbell rang. The Beverly Hills Hotel rooms have doorbells! Class.

It was room service with a bottle of Pinch scotch and a tray of shrimp cocktail.

"I didn't order this," I said to the waiter.

"It's courtesy of Mr. Greshler." He left.

Right, I thought to myself. Nice ploy, Abby. Trying to soften me up for the negotiations, huh? Like that will work!

So I enjoyed my scotch and shrimp, got a good night's sleep, and awoke ready for the battle that lay ahead.

I went to the Palm Court, gave my name, and was told they were expecting me and would show me to Mr. Greshler's table.

As I sat waiting, I scanned the room. I only recognized Marty Allen and Steve Rossi sitting across from me with a couple of other people. Allen and Rossi were an old comedy duo I remembered as a kid from the *Ed Sullivan Show*. But it was a star sighting nonetheless. Exciting even for a New Yorker.

And I waited. And waited.

I called over the waiter.

"Excuse me, do you have any idea where Mr. Greshler is? I have to leave shortly to catch my flight back. Has he called?"

"No. I'm sure he'll be here. Can I get you some more coffee?"

"No thanks," I responded. At that point, I'd had about five cups and was wired.

Finally, Abby arrived and as he sauntered over to his table, he stopped along the way to say hello to two people I assumed were celebrities in the room. With the exception of Allen and Rossi, I didn't recognize anyone. After giving his good wishes to them, he sat down.

"I'll be with you in a minute," he said. "Waiter, bring me a phone."

The waiter was there in seconds with a phone.

Abby dialed a number and while he was waiting for the other end of the line to answer, he dumped a bunch of pills out of a plastic bottle onto the table.

"Yes? Doctor? Good. Now remind me which one of these pills I'm supposed to take. OK. The red and blue one. OK. Goodbye."

Abby separated a red and blue pill from the collection, put the rest of the pills back in the bottle, threw the two left in his mouth, and gulped down some water. Done. Then he turned to me.

"You look younger that I thought you'd be. How old are you?"

I felt like responding: "And you look a lot older to me. I'd guess about 101. Those pills keeping you alive?"

"I'm thirty-four, Abby. And thanks for the scotch and shrimp. That was very nice. How did you know I drink Pinch scotch?"

"Junior, I'm paid to know such things." I later found out he'd called my assistant in New York while I was in the air and asked her what I liked to drink and eat. I guess she gets paid to tell people that.

"Well, thank you anyway. I'm afraid we need to move this along quickly. I have a flight that I must catch and can't stay too long. But I don't think there's much left to discuss."

"Yeah, sure. We'll get to it."

I was then regaled for the next hour and a half with story after story of deals Abby had done. Talk about an ego. But he was fascinating. He was the agent for Jerry Lewis and Dean Martin and was credited for putting the two of them together. I'd later learn that Abby was a legend and considered one of the best agents Hollywood ever saw. To me that morning, however, he seemed like an old curmudgeon who was wasting my time.

I interrupted, "Abby, I'd love to hear more of your stories but that will have to be another day. I have to go soon and we need to finish the deal."

He gave me a nasty look and said, "OK junior, here's what I want."

Most of what he asked for was fine. But he was way off on the money. The budget I'd been given was tens of thousands below his demand. He was so far over the budget that making a counteroffer seemed silly. I remember thinking that my client was sorely mistaken if it thought it was going to sign up the pair.

Nonetheless, I made a counteroffer below the budget I'd been given.

"You can't be serious? You don't get Randall and Klugman for that kind of price. Do better."

A waiter arrived.

"Mr. Wood, your car is waiting outside to take you to the airport whenever you're ready."

I was not about to miss my flight. And I'd had enough of Abby Greshler.

"Abby, I think you're right. We're too far apart. I'll go back to New York and give my client the bad news. Perhaps we'll talk again after that. It was wonderful meeting you."

I got up and started walking to the front door of the hotel.

As I left the Palm Court, I heard Abby bellow behind me, "Hey, Junior. No one walks away from Abby Greshler." I ignored him and kept walking. I had a plane to catch. He kept following, barking. I wasn't listening.

When I got to the driveway, awaiting me was one of the longest limos I'd ever seen. And the chauffer greeting me resembled a Playboy bunny more than a driver. She opened the giant trunk and offered to take my carry-on bag. I was mesmerized. And fantasizing. I was certainly not paying attention to Abby, who was now screaming at me.

I came back to my senses.

"Abby, I didn't realize you were following me." That's the only excuse I could think of after ignoring him.

"I don't follow anyone. And my last offer is . . ."

The number he asked for was only seventy-five percent of my budget! Somewhere between the table and the limo he'd come down more than fifty percent from his first demand.

I stared at him, having trouble processing what he'd said.

"That's my final offer, Junior. Take it or leave it."

"I'll take it."

So one of the most successful negotiations I ever conducted was the result of ignoring the agent and gawking at a limo and a breathtaking driver.

Hollywood.

chapter 23
Merry Christmas!
Enjoy the Spinal Cord.

Nicolae Ceaușescu was the leader and president of the Socialist Republic of Romania. He took over in 1965. On December 25, 1989, he and his wife, Elena, were executed following an impromptu and staged trial. This opened Romania for foreign investment. Other former Soviet satellite countries followed suit as the Soviet Union disintegrated.

I saw this as an opportunity.

I called in an associate and told him to get me demographic information on the Eastern European countries so I could decide which one held the best prospects as an outpost for the firm so it could sow in millions as the economies in the now free nations exploded. A pure capitalist move in the former communist enclaves.

A week passed and no word. I called him in again. "Where's the information on the countries I wanted?"

"I'm having trouble finding information."

A real genius, I thought.

"Well, look up the various Chambers of Commerce for the countries and ask them for the information." Duh.

Another week went by. No information. I called him in again.

"What's the problem? Where is the information I asked for?"

"I tried to find the Chambers of Commerce for those countries but there aren't any. They don't exist."

"Really?" I responded. "I'll tell you what. Form them. Form one for Romania, Bulgaria, and the rest. Then we can approach their consulates at the UN and see where that leads us."

So that's what we did. We formed about five new Chambers of Commerce, including the Romanian and Bulgarian Chambers of Commerce, and registered the names as trademarks at the U.S. Patent & Trademark Office in Washington, DC.

A few weeks passed and we got a call from the State Department.

"Why did you register all those trademarks for Eastern European Chambers of Commerce?"

I decided to be honest. "Well, to tell you the truth, we did it because we hope to find a way to take advantage of their new economies and make some money."

"Really?"

"Really."

"OK. Perhaps we can help. We'll set up some meetings for you with representatives of the various countries on your list."

We eventually met with folks from Romania, Bulgaria, and Georgia. The Bulgarians were very scary looking. Not nice. The Georgians didn't seem to have a clue. But the Romanians were warm and friendly. So they won the beauty contest.

To get us started, I asked one of my partners to visit Romania and see what it was like. He came back with a mixed report but a promising outlook. I then approached my brother, Gil, who at the time wasn't really doing much. I offered him a job to move to Romania and set up shop for us. He said he'd go for up to six months but no more.

When he arrived, our friends from Romania had already provided our first local lawyer, Victor. And we found an office.

At the time, there was no meaningful banking system and no credit cards. My brother had to pay everything in the local currency, the leu (pronounced "lay"). Inflation was off the Richter scale and he literally carried a suitcase full of leu, spending it quickly and buying more on the black market. Totally insane. But he was having fun.

Then I got another call.

"Mr. Wood, this is John Doe [not his real name]. I'm from the CIA. I'd like to talk to you about what you're doing in Romania."

"Right. John Doe from the CIA. Who is this really?"

"That's what I thought you'd say. So I'll tell you what. I'm going to hang up and you call the CIA on your own and ask for me." He hung up.

I called and asked for him.

He answered the phone. *Shit*, the CIA is watching me!

"OK, now that we have who I am out of the way, how can we help you in Romania? We have contacts there that can probably help you build the business."

"Right. And in exchange for what? You guys are spies."

He then went on about how this had nothing to do with spying. All the CIA wanted to do was help U.S. businesses succeed in the newly freed countries.

I told him that his offer was nice but we weren't interested. He said, "Fine," and hung up.

After a few more months, business grew and we were

actually making a few bucks. My brother decided to stay. He was enjoying himself. It was like the Wild West. He did point out, however, that it was likely the offices were bugged, but that was apparently true everywhere. And he didn't seem to mind that the electricity and water usually went off a few times a day. He was a pioneer.

I finally decided to visit Gil and flew over to Romania with my friend Arnie. When the plane landed, a limo came up to the gangway and my brother bounded up the stairs and waved for us to follow him to the car. Everyone else on the plane was told to stay in their seats.

Feeling like bigshots, we got in the limo, picked up our bags, and drove out of the airport in record time. Damn, I thought, it looks like Gil is really connected. No wonder he wants to stay.

"Before we go to the hotel, I'm taking you to meet Iliescu." Ion Iliescu was the President of Romania and our client.

While the meeting was short, it was the first time I'd ever met a president of a country.

The next day, we went to the office. When asked by a member of the staff if there was anything we'd like to experience while in Romania, I responded, "Yes. I'd like to have a typical meal you'd serve on Christmas to celebrate the day during the worst days of Communism."

Her look said "Is this idiot kidding?" but she nodded and said she'd take care of it.

That night, we sat down to dinner. The appetizer was tripe soup. The main course was braided, deep-fried cow spinal cord. The dessert was coffee and a doughnut. That's it. That was their Christmas meal. It was sad.

She then explained how terrible it was living under the

iron fist of Nicolae Ceaușescu. He limited citizens to no more than nine hundred calories a day. They had to hide enough additional food to get the calories they needed. He confiscated all the meats and other salable commodities, so most of their meals were dominated by organ meats. They were allowed one lightbulb. They were required to turn in anyone who was against the state, including their brothers, sisters, and parents if need be. Very often, people would simply disappear. And this was all happening in the 1980s, while we in America were enjoying just about anything we wanted.

I realized how incredibly uninformed I was. Completely naive. That visit and that meal opened my eyes to appreciate what we have and how awful it can be even in modern times, when such things seem too harsh to believe. But they were reality. And they continue to happen all over the world.

A number of years later, the local Romanian bar association convinced the government that Western firms with ex-pats needed to have a foreign partner admitted to Romania to stay in business. It was an effort to drive out foreign competition. I assumed that meant we'd have to close the office.

Not. My brother managed to get me admitted by presidential proclamation. So that brief visit with Iliescu proved to be very profitable. I remain a member of the Bucharest bar to this day.

My brother is still in Romania. He eventually bought the practice from us and continues working to make his and other lives better every day.

belvedere

chapter 24
The Story of a Lifetime

Eddie Phillips

Ten years in someone's life can pass quickly even though the voyage through it is punctuated by exhilarating highs and painful lows. In such journeys, the pleasant moments fade too quickly. This is the story of such a journey. A story about good times and bad. About friendships made and relationships forged.

Whatever individual lessons there are to be drawn from the journey remain with those who lived it. As for those who now read about it, the lessons are perhaps among stories retold through the blue haze of faded memories.

It is not a story of good versus evil or right versus wrong. That would be too easy. Too stereotypical.

Nor is it a story about defeat or victory. Like so much else in life, it was all a mixture of victories and defeats. Trying to neatly characterize any moral in this part of my life is an exercise with no purpose. What does matter is that the journey gave me the chance to live like few ever do; to play on a stage where your performance matters.

The story is about making decisions and reacting to the consequences, at times in a brilliant way; at other times idiotically. It's also about friendships forged in the business equivalent

of foxholes that got everyone through the firestorms. Friendships that are sealed in battle and that never fade. Friendships
that were the glue that kept the players together.

In late 1995, I received a call from the CFO of an advertising agency headquartered in Minneapolis, Minnesota. He
related that he and the chairman of the agency had a good
friend, Eddie Phillips, who had a minor trademark problem.
Unhappy with his current legal counsel, Eddie had asked them
for a referral. Obviously, I said I'd be happy to help.

Eddie called and suggested we get together in New York
to see if our chemistry worked and whether I thought there was
any value I might add to solutions Eddie needed. While the
approach seemed a bit too "California" for my taste, I figured
nothing would be lost by at least meeting him.

We finally met for dinner at the Monkey Bar on Fifty-fifth
Street in New York City. Lots of small talk. We finally got to
business as the evening ended.

Eddie was about to introduce Belvedere vodka into the
United States as the first super-luxury vodka, with a selling
point at retail of more than ten dollars above the most expensive
brands then available. Eddie related to me that his company,
Phillips Beverage Company, had spent nearly a year and almost
a million dollars conducting pre-market research. He was convinced that the product would be a success. But he had two
problems. First, a small winery in California had a United States
registered trademark for "Belvedere" for wine. Second, a small
company in France that was supplying the bottles for Belvedere
vodka was trying to interfere with the market by importing
similar-looking bottles. He'd been told by his former legal counsel that the winery should not be a problem. I characterized that
advice as some of the worst I'd ever heard. As for the French

company, he wanted to discuss options to deal with the problem and protect his market. Unfortunately, he had no contract with them. Nor was he very clear about the contract he had with the Polish distillery that made Belvedere vodka. What was very clear was that Eddie had anything but a "small" trademark problem. I was tempted to tell him that night that he was about to be in a nightmare, but I feared that level of pessimism might lose the account.

He explained that the key to Belvedere's success was first that it was distilled numerous times to assure true purity and an absolute minimum of the particulates found in distilled spirits that are a major case of hangovers. Second, the back of the Belvedere bottle was etched with a depiction of the Belvedere Palace in Warsaw, opposite a clear window on the other side of the bottle that created a very elegant and magnified perspective of the palace. The process to make the bottles was the same one used to make very expensive perfume bottles. The only place they could be made was in France because of environmental issues. It seems the etching process is not terribly kind on the ecosystem. But it sure was a beautiful bottle that would help sales.

We continued talking about one thing after another. Family. Politics. Values. We bonded and I left that evening with a new client. Little did I know how these two protagonists—a California winery and a French bottle broker—would forever change my life, and the lives of so many others.

It wasn't surprising that Eddie was such a character. His mother was Abigail Van Buren—Dear Abby. Throughout his entire life, he was schooled by his parents in what was right, not necessarily what might work or give someone an unfair advantage over a lesser competitor.

Of the many words of wisdom that Eddie used to say, I fondly remember one in particular: "Judge a man by the footsteps he leaves, not the promises he makes." There's barely a day that goes by when I don't think of those words.

About Your Fees

When we finished dinner at the Monkey Bar and were enjoying an after-dinner drink or two, Eddie brought up my fees.

Great, I thought, *I haven't even begun to do any work and he's already looking for a discount.* Maybe that's a Minneapolis thing. I prepared for the worst.

"So, Doug, how about instead of paying you your hourly fees, you instead take 25 cents per bottle of Belvedere I sell in perpetuity?"

Interesting, I thought. Here's this guy who is crazy enough to think people are going to pay more than $40 a bottle for frickin' vodka. Worse, he had a serious trademark problem and a marauding French adversary that appeared to have no morals. To even begin to fix the mess would mean hundreds of hours of work by at least a half dozen lawyers from my firm. In my informed opinion, the prospects of success were just too low to warrant a contingency arrangement.

But I wanted to be honest with him and give him the option to reconsider retaining me if he was looking more for a partner and outside counsel.

"Eddie, thank you for the offer, but to be honest with you and with all due respect, I'm just not convinced people will pay that much for vodka. I also think your issues are so complex that you would not want your legal counsel's advice to be influenced by a conflict between what was best for you and what might put more money in the pockets of my firm. So if you're still interested in retaining me, I'd prefer we go forward with billing on an hourly basis."

He immediately responded, "OK. While I think you're wrong, I'm happy to pay you hourly."

During the month that ensued, I had to fly to Paris to meet with local counsel I wanted to retain to help address the problems associated with the local bottle broker. I flew over first class on American Airlines, took a taxi to the Sofitel hotel across the street from the very chic Hôtel de Crillon, and got to work. Upon returning, I sent Eddie our first bill with the out-of-pocket expenses itemized in the normal fashion. Eddie called me.

"Doug, I got your invoice for the trip to Paris and I'd like to talk to you about it."

Here we go, I thought. He's going to complain about the first bill I've sent. I felt that knot in my stomach that lawyers always feel when a client is about to shortchange them on hard work because that's what you do to lawyers and their fees.

But I'd been there before so I just sucked it up, prepared to deal with his stinginess as best I could.

"Sure, Eddie. Is there a problem with the bill?"

"Yes. I see you flew first class, took taxis, and stayed at the Sofitel."

"Yes, Eddie. It's a long flight and I had to hit the ground running. So I decided to go first class." I assumed flying in the front of the plane was the source of the impending shave he intended to administer on my invoice.

"I know. But you're now working for the company that makes the most expensive vodka in the world and you need to travel in that fashion. Next time, you take the Concorde and you stay at the Ritz or some other five-star hotel. And you hire a limo to take you where you want to go."

Huh? I thought I had entered the Twilight Zone. Was this guy for real? Yes, he was.

So I flew the Concorde more than fifteen times, stayed at the finest hotels in the world, and enjoyed a driver just about wherever I went.

What follows will strain belief, but it's all true. Names, of course, have been changed where appropriate to protect both the innocent and the guilty.

Woes in Warsaw

Day One

As I strode down the jetway after a Lot Airline flight from Paris to Warsaw with a consultant (let's call him Peter) working with me on the Belvedere vodka case, the feeling was one of celebration. In two days, I managed to obtain incriminating evidence against the bottle manufacturers that was vital to the case and concluded two productive meetings in Paris, the world's most beautiful city. My only regret was the rain and freakish storms battering Europe, making getting around in Paris more like the harried hustle of New York rather than the relaxed pace of the Champs Elysée.

I was quite excited, having never been to Warsaw before. A seasoned world traveler, I had never become so jaded as not to love the adventure of a new city, particularly one that was formerly a part of my beloved country's enemy and Cold War heathens. Memories came back to me of the bleak and squalid streets of Bucharest, where I "enjoyed" the meal of tripe and spinal cord, imagining a very stupid and incontinent cow resembling a large slug.

A private driver picked us up at the airport and whisked us off in a Volvo to the posh Bristol Hotel, ensconced in a beautiful part of the city where post-war Polish workers rebuilt a Warsaw devastated by Hitler's heartless bombs of World War II.

Check-in was my first sign of impending danger, although I barely noticed. As I had done so many times in my well-traveled life, I whipped out my Platinum American Express card to check in, anxious to build up those frequent flyer miles so that I could bring my in-laws up from Florida to ruin another holiday sometime in the future.

Peter, the consultant, said, "You don't need that. You're in Poland."

Odd, I thought, but what the hell. When in Poland, act like a Polack.

Off to our rooms the consultant and I went. Peter had two yet-unread messages in his well-manicured hands.

As we approached the etched glass elevator in the lobby atrium, Peter suggested that we meet later in the bar for a drink. While I was of course reluctant to have a drink since it was already near midnight, I felt compelled to accept, knowing it would be my first opportunity to learn some of the history of Warsaw I so fervently desired to know.

The bellman was at the door of room 511 before I even got there, luggage ready, waiting to give me the key.

The room was magnificent. Large and well equipped. Before I could unpack, turn-down service arrived in the person of a beautiful chambermaid. My thoughts wandered, but being the married man I was, they soon returned to the task at hand—

the first steps in an effort to preserve Poland's vodka and the rest of the world from the unwarranted intrusions of a group of French pirates.

Then the call came that shattered the pristine night.

It was Peter.

"I'll see you in the bar," I cheerfully said as I picked up the phone.

"No," said Peter with an unusual tremor in his usually steel-lined voice. "Stay in your room and I'll be there in a minute. We need to talk."

Undaunted by the impending complications, I continued unpacking, trying to figure out how to get my third arm—my Macintosh PowerBook 5300cs, fully loaded with the latest in communications software—to work on the Bristol Hotel's telephone system. I needed to be connected to the real world.

I greeted Peter upon hearing the knock on the door.

"Sit down," suggested Peter with a hint of insistence in his voice. "We have a problem."

His words immediately brought to my mind those immortal words by one of my hero astronauts: "Houston, we have a problem." But I still didn't worry. After all, I was not on the way to the moon and Peter certainly wasn't a NASA-trained astronaut, although his haircut was somewhat reminiscent of the brave astronaut who saved the space program with his singular talents and bravado.

"We may be in danger," he said, noticeably shaken.

"What do you mean, 'danger'?" I asked. "Are you suggesting physical danger?" Warsaw was rapidly losing its romantic appeal, and the idea of a fast flight to freedom started to simmer in the back of my mind.

"I spoke to Rosanna," he said. "She feels she's in danger

and intimated we may be as well."

Rosanna was a local source we were told had evidence that would help us in our fight with the French.

Peter continued, "She now 'remembers' new things that she didn't say on Monday. Her story has changed. Rosanna feels threatened that she'll be a scapegoat. What do you think we should do?"

I had the urge deep in my stomach to say, "What should we do? You're asking me? What do I look like, the Shell Answer Man? This is your country, pal. You figure it out." But instead, I calmly asked, "Gee, Peter, do you really think we're in physical danger?"

The "yes" from Peter came all too quickly.

"OK," I responded as my stomach knotted. "Let's go over our options."

It was interesting that the first memory that came to me was the time I was with my friend Arnie, traveling in Transylvania with my brother, Gil. On that dark night, Gil was stopped in a backwoods town by some very nefarious-looking policemen for driving the wrong way on a one-way street. As they asked Gil to get out of the car, Arnie leaned over to me and said in his typical deadpan way, "As far as I'm concerned, they're putting the electrodes on your balls first." An odd first thought.

I advised Peter, "We can, one, do nothing; two, change rooms; or three, check out and go to another hotel." I intentionally failed to suggest the fourth alternative of getting the hell out of Dodge. But I didn't want Peter to perceive my mounting fear.

"There's no point to going to another hotel," said Peter. "They can find us in whatever hotel we go."

Perfect, I thought. The whole damn country has a hotel

directory that lists the whereabouts of every foreigner trying to save the Polish economy from collapse. Another example of global ingrates.

"I will call security and tell them our lives are in danger. We will change rooms and vanish. We will vanish in this hotel. Only the hotel manager will know where we are," suggested Peter.

Great idea, I thought. *Our lives are in danger and Peter's only suggestion is that we vanish in a former police state that lacks any hotel where we could hide. Wouldn't that make it easier to hide the bodies?*

So Operation Vanish began. Funny how the word "vanish" reminded me of a toilet bowl cleaner and being flushed to oblivion.

The hotel's night manager arrived. He moved us to a secret floor of the hotel, a floor that was "out of service." I wondered how a whole floor could be out of service, but decided asking logical questions was not a particularly good idea at this time.

After arriving at my new room, one considerably smaller than my first room, we were joined by yet another manager.

Peter immediately started a discussion in Polish, so I didn't understand a word. Instead, I was on the phone with my client, Eddie Phillips, trying to get the idea across to Eddie that strange things were under way. As I concluded my conversation with Eddie, he graciously asked, "Is there anyone you'd like me to call?" I wasn't sure if I should suggest my next of kin or the governor.

"No," I replied. "There's no one you need to call."

Peter then informed me that the hotel wanted to call the police.

Shit, I thought. Here come the electrodes.

Peter and I quickly agreed that calling the police wasn't

such a good idea. So after talking to the two managers, it was agreed that Peter and I would sign a statement attesting to the fact that the police were not called because Peter and I didn't want them called. I drafted what seemed more like a death warrant than a release. We signed it and gave it to the managers, hoping the night's turmoil was finally coming to an end.

Trying to relax, I asked the manager if he could get me something to eat, a bottle of vodka, and some ice. After all, I couldn't go to the bar anymore since I wasn't really there and I couldn't have a scotch from the mini bar straight up. He consented and the two managers left.

Peter and I remained, lamenting the change in the course of day in such a short period of time.

The next knock on the door should have been the ice. It wasn't.

The pair of managers, now beginning to look like Siamese twins joined at the hip, re-entered the safe room, a nice plate of fruit and salmon in hand, but no ice or vodka. They reported that yet another manager was now in the picture and was insisting on calling the police.

I couldn't help but wonder just how many managers the Bristol had, anyway. I ate the salmon, wondering if it was my last meal, and politely reminded the brain-dead messengers that I still wanted vodka and ice.

Peter got on the phone with the unseen manager, a man Peter would learn was French. While Peter persuaded the invisible manager to not call the police, I took the time to get to know a little more about the manager at the door. I learned that the hotel had an "incident" the previous year, which was why the mystery uber-manager was concerned. I elected not to ask for any details on the "incident."

Peter succeeded in his task. The police would not be called. Finally, a victory for our fearless duo of missing businessmen.

The managers left and Peter went off to his own secret room.

Alone, my thoughts wandered. Where, I can't remember. They just plain wandered.

It was now 3:00 a.m., just about the time murderous villains typically ply their trade in the naked cities of the world. I knew I needed sleep, but how would I know if an intruder with ill intent was about to ventilate my head—or other body parts—while I drifted through dreamland?

It was then I noticed the tin cover that had been on the plate of salmon. *Perfect*, I thought, and hatched my plan. I carefully balanced the tin cover atop the arms of the automatic door closer above the door to the room. Like a tin plate might knock out some 300-pound Polish assassin. But I had to do something. That done, I knew I also needed an escape route. So I opened the large window to the roof. While the roof was slightly sloping and made of shale, I decided it was the only way out. I figured that if I slipped and fell to my death on the pavement below, that was a better way to go than from an assassin's bullet or bayonet.

With the tin cover above the door and the window open and ready, I went to bed and turned on CNN. After about two minutes, the station was lost, only fuzz appearing on the screen. I moved it to the next station, BBC. It lasted two minutes and vanished. This went on until there were no more stations that worked except some German station that looked like it had a bunch of ex-Nazis lamenting the demise of the Reich. Finally, I began to fall asleep at about 4:00 a.m., only to be awakened every five minutes by a creak in the building or a harmless shadow through the window.

As I dozed off, the tin plate fell and clanged on the floor. I jumped out of bed. My heart was nearly beating out of my chest. That's when the first shot hit me. Not a bullet, but a fucking pigeon that had flown into the room through the open window, and in a panic, flew right into me. Chaos ensued with me trying to bat at the pigeon and the pigeon flying like a lunatic. It seemed like an eternal battle for survival that probably only lasted a minute or two until my unwanted guest and assassin impersonator flew out the open window. Exhausted, with my heart still in overdrive, I closed the window, ignored the tin plate, and went back to bed.

Day Two

I got up at 8:00 a.m. and showered and dressed, remembering some of the shower scenes from James Bond flicks—or was it the shower scene from *Psycho*? Never mind.

At about 9:00 a.m., I gently knocked on Peter's door. Peter appeared, obviously just out of bed, wearing a nice pair of white PJs that resembled a funeral shroud. I was happy to see that he was also breathing. Peter said he was making phone calls and he'd meet me in the restaurant in about a half hour. "Don't worry," he said. "They don't know what you look like."

My breakfast was blessedly uneventful, although the coffee was a wee bit on the road tar side. Certainly, no one in the restaurant looked like a criminal, assuming I knew the telltale signs of a criminal in the first place.

Peter arrived, donning a snappy coat and tie, and reported to me that his phone no longer worked.

Great, no line to the outside world or 911.

Entering the lobby, the coast looked pretty clear. Awaiting us were a man I'll call Paul, my Polish lawyer counterpart, and a local bootlegger I'll call Waldo, the first of the bootleggers I would encounter. Peter and I elected not to tell the pair that they were walking with marked men.

While walking to the front door of the hotel, Peter secretly told me that he had met with the hotel manager and the two of them agreed that anyone who needed either of us should call and ask for Mr. Jones. "Fine," I whispered, "but how will they know which one of us is the Mr. Jones they want to talk to?" Peter agreed that was something he'd have to work out in the afternoon. I told him I wanted to be Mr. Johnson so I could say, in my last dying words, "You doesn't has to call me Johnson."

As we approached the smiling doorman, Peter graciously let Paul and Waldo go first. After all, you never know how trigger-happy the Polish Goodfellows might be. Following them through the door, the two of us were cautious, wondering if the red-jacketed bellman was really an assassin in disguise. Thankfully, our escape into the broad daylight of an open street went smoothly. Needless to say, Paul and Waldo were a little confused as to why we wanted to get in the car so fast. It did not please me in the slightest that I had to sit in the front passenger seat. Somehow, riding shotgun was not my idea of how to wander the streets of this former totalitarian state of paranoid military retirees.

Paul made a gallant effort to point out the sights as we maneuvered through the crowded streets of the rebuilt city. In truth, I didn't give a shit, partly because I couldn't see anything from my crouched position in the front seat and partly because I was barely awake to remember. Peter said a few words, too, conveniently safe between the cushioning bulletproofing of Paul and Waldo.

What a hero Peter was, letting a first-time visitor take the hit.

I began to wonder if this had anything to do with the fact that I was a lawyer, remembering that the only difference between a lawyer and a carp is that one is a bottom-feeding scum-sucker and the other is a fish.

The first stop was at the offices of the lawyers for Waldo, the bootlegger. I was told the building was formerly the Embassy of Mongolia but the law firm got it for a steal when the marauding country of murderers went bust (or something like that).

I felt it made perfect sense to have lawyers moving into the former haunts of a bunch of Mongolian marauders.

I was sure there'd be no bugs inside to eavesdrop on our conversations, except maybe a few thousand receivers implanted in the walls connected to the central headquarters of the former Soviet Supreme where a bunch of ex-Commies had nothing better to do than listen to Westerners thinking they were alone. Paranoid? Maybe.

The first room we were put in had a cheap table and a bunch of chairs. No paintings. No plants. No nothing. It's probably easier to clean up the blood that way, I speculated as my eyelids began to droop somewhere between my chin and shoelaces. The four of us sat down, awaiting the arrival of Professor Topple (not her real name), a lawyer from Krakow, a three-hour train ride away. I hoped the trains ran on time since another innocent party in the room might crowd the scope of the rifle, and the shooter might have a grudge against women.

As I waited, I toyed with the idea of writing "She's a Bitch" on a piece of paper and leaning it against the window when no one was looking. But I decided not to since most assassins were the macho kinda guys who would know anyway.

Topple arrived, strangely impersonating a troll. Nice disguise, I thought. Boy, what a letdown when I realized she *was* a troll. A troll lawyer. First one I'd ever seen. Bad news, though, since trolls are good luck and the sniper would probably mistake her for a floor lamp.

The first of many cups of undrinkable coffee arrived as the group set about trying to understand a series of events that made nuclear fission seem like explaining a ham sandwich. Hour after hour passed, everyone alive but probably better off dead. Then with no warning, one of the attorney's assistants barged in to announce the room must be used by someone else, so the group had to pick up their papers and move to another room.

Who the hell would want this piece of shit conference room? I wondered. I couldn't wait to see the condition of the next one.

We picked up our papers and wandered across the lobby as the troll lawyer directed us into a room with a small table and two chairs. That was fine with me so long as the troll didn't sit on my lap. Exhibiting her first sign of intelligence, Topple the Troll observed that we wouldn't all fit in that room. No shit, Sherlock, I thought, now nearly comatose from lack of sleep. The thought crossed by mind, however, that my fatigued state was a blessing since I wouldn't feel a thing if my chest or head became Polish graffiti.

So we moved to yet another room, one identical to the room we first used. Same size. Same lack of decoration, except for a calendar on the wall from the firm's travel agent. I made a mental note to see the partner who was in charge of decorating the offices to get some pointers on using artwork provided by suppliers. I also felt a yearning (luckily not when I was looking at the troll lawyer) to meet the idiot who wanted the other conference room so badly that he evicted us in the first place. Shoot, I thought, using a rather inappropriate word for the moment, the other client must be a real big deal. Maybe a child molester or something.

Finally, we settled in and began our journey through insanity once again. After a while, sure that everyone had a headache, I decided it was time to delegate responsibility among the Polish lawyers. So I told Paul to get a copy of Topple the Troll's files and review them for me and Peter. After five hours of listening to the troll try to explain circumstances that would have even made Lee Harvey Oswald confess, it was time to go. Sitting there knowing my client was paying for worthless advice drove me nuts. I couldn't stand it. Or her.

Outside, the incessant rain continued, making me all the more concerned. It just plain felt like death was in the air. Besides, people can hide all sorts of harmful implements under bulky rainwear, and their fingerprints don't stay on a wet trigger or the handle of a twenty-inch butcher knife.

Paul announced it was time to get something to eat. It was my first lesson on the eating habits of Poles. There are no habits. They eat indiscriminately throughout the day. It was 3:00 p.m. and Paul suggested we get lunch. He suggested the Actor's Restaurant down a dirty, dingy, dampened street. A perfect shooting field.

The restaurant was my first encounter with a local bistro. I was thrilled to finally eat some real Polish food.

Upon entering, I first noticed that the place was nondescript, walls festooned with dusty old pictures of long-dead actors. Perhaps it was decorated by the same guy who bought the travel agent calendars for the troll's law firm.

We were brought to a table in a room that was lit about as

brightly as a medieval dungeon, which was fine with me. Darkness made targets harder to see except in close-up work. And if someone got too close, I could always look at Paul and Waldo and say, "Hi, Doug and Peter," to buy time.

Surprisingly, Peter sat with his back to the door. Pretty daring. But it was too late to say anything before Peter put himself into harm's way. I figured if Peter took one in the back of the head, I would be sure to deliver a glowing eulogy for the hero, so long as his estate paid my cleaning bill for Peter's brains on my suit. Actually, I felt some trepidation at the thought, hoping that we'd at least get our meal before Peter lost his head.

But fortunately, the meal progressed without incident. I let Peter order for me, figuring he'd order something really good, being Polish and all that. Then Peter ordered something different for himself. Oh well, I figured there was probably lots of good stuff on the menu.

After some reasonable soup, the main course arrived, a plate of minute steak on a bed of overcooked instant rice covered in a sauce Chef Boyardee would have rejected as inferior even for canned food. It was accompanied by a nice helping of overcooked stir-fried vegetables and about a ton of broccoli, the first sign I would see that broccoli was a national pastime in Poland. No wonder George Bush never made it to Poland. Peter had a really good-looking plate of pork. The only thing that made the meal tolerable was the Chopin vodka.

Peter decided to call Rosanna so she could come to the restaurant and talk with Paul about a meeting with Barbara, another informant, that past Monday. He left the room. While Peter was at the telephone, I decided to relate the story of the night before to Paul so that I could be reassured that there was really nothing to worry about. After I finished, Paul suggested,

"We'd better be careful and take the threat seriously. Warsaw can be a pretty dangerous place at times."

Whoa! I thought. Just as a few vodkas start to take the edge off my fear of dying in a flood of my own precious body fluids, this lawyer from Warsaw tells me I should take it seriously.

All at once, Peter's absence became a source of considerable consternation. Should I look for him and risk walking right into a gangland execution? Or should I wait, sitting like a pigeon on a limb? Or was that a dope on a rope?

Finally, I decided to stretch my legs and considered sitting at another table with a bunch of people quacking in Polish. I figured if anyone is looking for two men, then Paul and Waldo will fit that bill.

But just as I was about to rise from my chair, Peter reappeared, bounding for the table and his plate of really good food that sat next to my plate of really bad food.

"Rosanna is on her way," announced Peter as he put his fork into another piece of his succulent meal on the plate beside my really unsucculent meal.

We sat and ate. And ate. And ate. Until there was nothing left. I wondered if they sold Tums in Poland. Then we sat and waited. And waited. And waited. Peter called Rosanna's office. She was not there. By 5:00 p.m., it was too late to wait any longer, so we left, only to bump into the tardy Rosanna on the street. After obligatory hellos, Peter, Paul, Rosanna and I took a cab, first dropping Peter and me off at the Bristol.

I went to my secret room to relax before I planned to have about two hundred vodkas in the bar. I figured resting a few minutes would make it easier to pace myself at the bar, at least through the first fifty shots. Then the phone rang.

It was another call from Peter asking me to come downstairs, this time because Barbara was there to deliver her story.

I found the two in the dimly lit lobby. I figured that maybe it's just a general precaution around this country to keep public places dark. Peter was reading a written statement as Barbara sat uncomfortably on an adjacent couch wearing a coat and hat that would make an Eskimo jealous, even though it was fifty degrees outside. What was with the Nanook of the North look?

Upon my approach, Peter introduced me in English, so I assumed she wouldn't have any idea who I was. That may have been why she wouldn't make eye contact with me. I really don't like it when someone doesn't make eye contact with me.

"What's the statement say?"

Peter told me what I expected to hear until he got to the part where Barbara said she was scared for her personal safety.

"Huh? Exactly what does she mean by scared for her personal safety?"

Peter spoke to her in Polish and told me her fear had something to do with her personal health.

Well, yeah. At this point, the translation game was getting really stale. In one frickin' day, three more people get added to the hit list: the local lawyer, the bootlegger, and an Eskimo impersonator, I thought. This was getting to be like a real United Nations deal.

Barbara said she had nothing else to say and she and Peter bid me a fond farewell.

As she left, I said, "May the wind be in your sails and the ocean beneath your feet. Don't worry that you're on the *Titanic*." I guess it was a good thing she didn't speak English.

Peter then left and went to the first of his private meetings without me. But that didn't worry me. I knew in my heart that Peter would never sell me down the river just to save his own ass. After all, he was Polish and I was Irish. A pair who could trust one another. Right.

I finally made it to the bar, ready to pace out the evening in style. I surveyed the stock on the bar much like James Bond and settled on a twelve-year-old Macallan on ice. The bartender asked me if I wanted a double. "No thanks," I said. When the drink came, I first thought that the glass was one from the last customer who left some residue in the bottom of the glass until I finally understood why the bartender asked me if I wanted a double. "Shit," I muttered. "Isn't anything going to go right?" But my inner voice reminded me to stop bitching. I was still alive, right?

From then on, the droplets of scotch tasted pretty good.

Now relaxed, I gently took one of my precious cigars, a Padron 1994 Anniversario Exclusivo, from my Pheasant leather case. After gingerly clipping the end of the handmade smoke with my precision Zino stainless steel double-edged cutter, I said to the bartender, "Give me a snifter of brandy—your cheapest stuff," now knowing how the system worked. Upon its arrival, I lovingly dipped the end of the cigar into the snifter, swirling it around the elixir to evenly soak its tender leaves and wrapper. I then held the Robusto softly in my hand as I lit the dry end with a Davidoff match to bring the beginnings of life to the dormant delicacy. After a few short puffs to be sure of an even light, I blew once on the lit end as the final touch to the affair and placed the pleasure back between my lips, sucking gently against its favorable brandy taste. I thought that maybe I should write a letter to *Playboy* magazine about it. What can I say? I like cigars. "And who said smoking a cigar wasn't better than sex," I asked myself. Yep, I'm definitely an Irishman. I like corned beef and cabbage, too!

After about an hour that I spent trying to determine just how many years of training in Poland it takes for a bartender to be able to pour one drop at a time out of a bottle, Peter returned and tapped me on the shoulder to introduce Lucas, aka "Wabash," aka "Wabash the Cannonball." It seems Wabash was some kind of middle minister without a portfolio who wanted to talk with Peter and me before our official first meeting with his boss, the director, the next morning. Pulled so unceremoniously back to reality, I put on my game face and moved to a table to receive the briefing.

Not much substance was relayed and I was in no mood to ask yet another Pole about my personal safety. I was too tired and figured it would just give me more indigestion anyway.

The meeting ended with a promise to meet one another the next day.

After putting a few chairs in front of the door to my room, since they took away my killer-detecting tin plate, I went to bed and watched television until about 4:00 a.m. This night, the TV worked and I got to watch CNN International reporters talk about events around the world that I couldn't have cared less about. I was alive, and that was enough for me.

Day Three

The morning sun awakened me from a dream I can't remember but knew was good. Real good. It had something to do with leather, but for the life of me, I just can't remember.

Later, I journeyed to the lobby in the clear-glassed elevator that gave any sniper a clear view from the passing floors. Since the glass was all around me, my jockeying as I tried to be behind someone else in the elevator did no good, but it gave me a sense of momentary security, albeit at the expense of the other guy.

After a breakfast of Polish sausage and eggs, the day began with a meeting with Wabash at the Ministry of the Treasury as the first shot across the bow of the French company we were there to fight. The place looked like a leftover from the Communist austerity program. Green-painted walls and dimly lit hallways, guys in uniforms who looked like they didn't have a clue what they were doing. Wabash waved to a couple of them and we didn't have to go through any security check. If you ever want to blow up the Ministry of the Treasury, just kidnap some bureaucrat and make them wave to the security guards.

Since we were there early in hopes of getting the meeting started on time, we were forced to sit in a cramped, dingy hallway until the director was ready to see us. Finally, after cooling our heels for about a half hour, we were ushered into the director's office, a small, dirty, dark, and grimy place. I immediately knew this guy was a waste of time.

After about a half hour, the meeting had deteriorated into a Polish language shouting match, none of which I understood. I was just waiting for someone to take off their shoe and pound the table like Nikita Khrushchev did in the United Nations when he vowed to bury capitalism. (Nice try, Nikita. Look where it got you, you dead asshole.)

The tension calmed and after about an hour, we took the first opportunity to bid this character farewell, leaving the director alone to convince himself of his own personal importance. But since he didn't have the guts to do a damn thing to help our cause, I figured the director must use very convincing mental masturbation to get through work every day.

It was at this point that I began to realize the formula for identifying the anatomy of a good businessman in Warsaw.

The formula is a variation of the Wizard of Oz. First, you

have to determine if the guy has any brain. This is difficult to do on short notice. Generally, you have to spend some time with them to determine whether they have a brain. Quality time on the Yellow Brick Road. Assuming, however, that you determine that they do indeed have a brain, you must then determine if they have any balls. Since I was not willing to reach into another man's pants, this proved to be a very difficult part of the test. Later, after a full week in Poland, I concluded that there must have been a whole lot of castrations during the Communist reign. Mind control. Since a person can't live if their brain is removed, the Commies must have figured that removing a guy's balls was just as effective. From what I could see, it worked. Then there was the final factor—the size of their office. At first, I thought the bigger a guy's office, the more likely he had balls. But I was told that new bureaucrats shunned the large office for the austerity and efficiency of the smaller office. That was said, however, by a guy who had a small office and who, I suspected, had no balls. And so the circular dilemma went. No brain. No balls. No office. No hope.

Undaunted, we moved to their next meeting, across town at the offices of yet another lawyer, Skubish, aka Darth Vader.

When I first met him, I knew this guy had all the equipment and looked the part as well. Sitting at the head of the ornate conference room table, Darth looked as if he were holding court over his collection of serfs. Of course, serfs with no balls.

Darth outlined the course of action. Slowly, he laid out his plan with an occasional suggestion by me. I was dangerously beginning to get into the game. It was a game of corporate hit men surgically removing pesky warts as though they were some old scabs that just wouldn't go away. But you knew in your heart that they'd come back. You know what that's like. They never really go away. So how good was this plan anyway?

Anyway, Darth had answers. Unfortunately, it turned out he didn't have the pocketbook. What a letdown. Here I thought I was about to make Starship Troopers look like a bunch of pansies and Darth turns out to be just another money-hungry lawyer. You know what those are like. Those oozy, opinionated ones that you just love to pick on. But they just won't go away, will they? Kinda like an old scab, if you get the idea.

So I made a deal. I'd have Eddie contribute some of his hard-earned money. Funny, I was finding it increasingly easy to spend Eddie's money. I figured I might not get out of the country alive so I might as well go down spending Eddie's money. Darth accepted and "Operation Up Yours, Frenchy" began.

Now beginning to get the idea, I told Paul in the cab back to the Bristol: "Trust no one." I told Paul, "Keep an eye on him."

"Sure, Doug," responded Paul. "But he is a professor and that might be a little awkward, if you know what I mean."

I suggested to Paul that some of the stupidest people I had ever met were professors. Paul hung his head, knowing that I would never understand. (I later learned he was a professor, too.)

Someday, Grasshopper, I will teach you, I thought as I looked at Paul.

As the cab continued on its journey into the night, I sat back and stared out of the window, trying to make out the faces of the forlorn pedestrians walking through the falling rain, and I wondered where I'd gone wrong.

After dropping off Paul, Peter and I went to our next rendezvous, this time at the Parliament building to meet once again with Wabash, the odd little man who just kept on showing up all over Warsaw.

We entered through the main entrance of the Parliament building, Peter carrying a big bag just about the right size for some really major plastic explosives or machine gun. We were greeted by two guards. Peter spoke to them in Polish, saying he had an appointment with the undersecretary. They looked confused. They looked at a directory. Peter continued to argue.

Great, I thought. We're in the seat of the Parliament, where the prime minister keeps his office, and Peter is arguing with a couple of goons carrying guns. And all that while Peter held that damn bag of his, close to his hip. Suddenly, the guards showed understanding and waved us on, never checking a thing. What the hell? Let bombers and terrorists in; it's only the center of the Polish government.

So we started wandering the halls of the building. Peter insisted he knew where he was going. After a few turns, guess who shows up? Wabash, ready to take us to the meeting. As we approach the end of the corridor, I saw yet another pair of guards. This time, they even had a walk-through metal detector. Then I got it: the tight security was inside. Lure the terrorist in and then make the arrest.

Wabash totally ignored the metal detector and Peter followed right behind him, thereby avoiding the three-alarm fire his bag should have caused if he'd gone through the detector alone. I knew I had nothing to hide so I bravely walked right through the detector, my chest thrust forward in American pride. The alarm immediately went off, alerting the gun-toting guards to a potential danger. I stopped, trying to find that place in my mind that I could use during a full body search to overcome the pain. One of the guards looked up, then back to his buddy.

Wabash looked back at me with a look that said, "What are you waiting for? Move your ass."

Man, I thought. I can't even make it as a terrorist. It also made me feel really good about the security in the building.

We proceeded into the office of the undersecretary and waited in his lobby. I noted that he had a very big office.

The undersecretary walked into the room and he was none other than Doogie Howser, MD. "For Christ's sake," I thought, "this guy's a frickin' teenager. He's probably too young to drink."

After being seated in Doogie's office, Peter told our tale of woe in fighting the French and Doogie nodded along. It's too bad Peter didn't begin the story with "Once upon a time." I figured Doogie might have liked the story even more.

Doogie's secretary, the secretary to the undersecretary, arrived with tea and coffee. That reminded me of yet another tradition I learned on this trip. Poles can't talk unless they have a cup of tea or coffee. Every meeting. Tea or coffee. At first, I asked for coffee. After about three cups of the tar, I decided to go with tea. It only took one cup to convince me that water was the only sensible alternative. As for Doogie, I wanted to suggest that the secretary to the undersecretary get Doogie a nice warm glass of milk.

Peter finished the story and Doogie asked Peter to call him back in a few days. I figured Doogie would want another story by then. I made a mental note to suggest to Peter that the next story for Doogie be "Dickski and Janeski, the Madcap Polskies," a lovely story of two young Poles who went up the hill and got blown away by a Russian mortar. A real tearjerker that Steven Spielberg would undoubtedly someday make into a movie.

Back into the hallways we went, free to wander wherever

we pleased. Peter suggested we try to find the prime minister's office, just for fun. I vetoed that idea, still believing that there had to be some kind of security in the Parliament. Peter only laughed.

Eventually, we found Wabash's office (how surprising!), where Peter bummed a ride back to the Bristol. This would be my first encounter with Wabash behind the wheel. It was on this ride that Wabash became "Wabash the Cannonball." To say this guy couldn't drive for shit was an understatement. Illegal U-turns in oncoming traffic? No problem. Rapid change of lanes without regard to other cars? No problem. Red lights? Wabash the Cannonball didn't need no stinkin' red lights. By the time we got to the hotel, I was convinced that Wabash was the hit man. Kinda like a kamikaze.

Peter went off to another secret meeting with some fellow Poles, this time with Romanoff and Wesolowski. It was dinner-ski at the Bristolski for the Polskies and I again found myself alone in the bar.

Being a social butterfly, I decided to make the best of my loneliness and befriend the new bartender, a nice guy who spoke English. I was just happy to hear someone speak my native language for a change.

Well, the two of us hit it off just fine. Buddy the bartender decided I should learn more about the drinks of Poland and took me on a liquid tour. From Bison vodka to honey liquor and drinks mixed with stuff Buddy said Poland couldn't export. The tour meandered through the distilleries of Poland as it wended its way along the highways and byways. The evening, and my mind, eventually faded away.

Day Four

The next morning, Peter and I met in the elevator en route to a meeting with Wesolowski.

"Where were you last night?" asked Peter.

"In the bar," I said quietly, so as not to contribute to the impending explosion in his head.

"Funny, I didn't see you when I left the restaurant."

That's no surprise, I thought. I was the guy on the floor eating bison grass. At least that's where I figured I must have been based on the taste in my mouth.

Luckily, I bounced back from the abyss as the elevator doors opened and I was introduced to Romanoff, aka "Mr. Fix," playing a role quite similar to Harvey Keitel's role in *Pulp Fiction*.

The three of us met in the business center. Half the time, Mr. Fix was on his cell phone telling someone to go stick it to themselves. As he drifted in and out of conversations with Peter and me, it became clear that this guy had a brain and I was pretty sure he had balls. Just the office factor was left undiscovered.

We adjourned, promising to get together again after Peter's and my next opportunity, a meeting that would prove to be the most important one we'd have. A meeting at the offices of the Center for Supreme Control, the most dreaded investigators in all of Poland.

Unlike with the other meetings, this time the supreme controller sent his car to fetch us; a spotless Alfa Romeo with a driver who unquestionably tore the wings off flies as a child. Flyboy sped through the city to the offices of the supreme controller, an imposing building in the center of town. As we followed the driver into the building, the first sight of its past reputation for pain was a huge staircase with the sign above it announcing you had entered the Chamber of the Supreme Controller. No kidding.

We were brought to the office of Wiesinski, who I later learned was Peter's dinner partner the night before. This guy had three gigantic offices! He also had two secretaries. This bastard was for real. Real as in it's real bad if you ever, ever, ever hear from him.

After some small talk that I barely remember because my mind kept conjuring up the unholy nights of torture that undoubtedly entertained the likes of Wiesinski during the cold Polish winters, we were escorted by one of his secretaries to the adjourning conference room. Waiting were three of his henchmen, aka the Three Musketeers, ready to listen to our tale. After sitting down and being offered the obligatory coffee, I wondered whether it might be a good idea to say Peter and I had made a mistake and we'd just be on our way. We were really looking for Diana Ross of the Supremes, not the supreme controller. No harm, no foul. But it was too late.

We talked. The Musketeers listened. They took notes. Wiesinski barked orders. I spilled my coffee. Finally, the meeting ended because Wiesinski had to go to another meeting. The Three Musketeers, Peter, and I remained seated while Wiesinski put on his coat. Once Wiesinski was gone, one of the Musketeers escorted Peter and me to a waiting cab. A dirty, dented cab. No more Alfa Romeo for the boys. No sir. Not necessary. We had already spilled the beans. Sung like canaries. Expendable. Meaningless.

We decided to seek refuge with Mr. Fix.

His office was large and modern. Quite understandable for a man of many identities. When we arrived, Mr. Fix greeted us like long-lost brothers. Just like the Mafia does to guys just before you have a clear view through their head made by a .45-caliber Excedrin.

"Coffee?" asked one of his secretaries.

"Screw coffee," said Peter. "Bring us whiskey."

And so Peter, Mr. Fix, and I sipped our whiskey and plotted our next moves. As the meeting wound to a close, Mr. Fix rummaged through his closet and found a box of Montecristos. He offered one to me and one to Peter and took one for himself. The only problem was that they were as dry as the Sahara, so I ordered that some brandy be brought in to dip the cigars. The three of us enjoyed the smoke; a smoke I would later learn was Peter's first cigar, and he didn't even gag.

Mr. Fix offered to share a cab back to the hotel.

On the way, the cab drove by a restaurant where Mr. Fix said he had an important meeting later that night. That struck me as suspicious. But then again, I was getting to the point where everything in Poland seemed suspicious.

Mr. Fix took us to his private apartment in the city. The apartment was in a dreary part of town that I figured would be the perfect place to have someone get permanently lost. It didn't make me feel any better as we walked up two flights in the dark hallway to get to the apartment. It reminded me of the scene from *The Godfather* when Clemenza walked up the stairs just before he riddled some dumb schmuck to oblivion.

When Mr. Fix opened the door, it was like an oasis. Wood trim and modern décor. Cable television. A big bed. A really big bed. And when Mr. Fix showed us that the refrigerator was stocked with nothing other than Champagne, it was obvious what he used this little unit for. I couldn't help but figure this must be the way Mr. Fix wants us to know he has balls.

Following the tour of Mr. Fix's brothel, the cab took us further into the bowels of the city until Mr. Fix left the cab and Peter and I went back to the Bristol. But the ever-clever Peter and I made a reservation at the very restaurant where Mr. Fix said he had his important meeting later that night. Quite the spies, huh?

When we showed up at the restaurant, sure enough, Mr. Fix was there. With a blond. A real number. Looks like just another night of Champagne from the fridge for Mr. Fix.

As sleep overtook me later that night, I felt more secure, knowing that Mr. Fix was in our corner. Or was he?

Day Five

I awakened to a sunny day, the first sunny day I'd seen all week.

At noon, we met Mr. Fix in the bar. He brought along Boris, a smarmy-looking cop drooling at the mouth for his next collar.

Boris listened to our tale, a tale I could even understand in Polish at that point, having heard it so many times. I wondered, briefly, if it was wise to be telling the story to everyone we met. But it was too late for that.

The meeting adjourned with Boris asking Peter to drop off papers at his office on Tuesday.

With the sun shining brightly and, I hoped, blinding any eyes peering through a gun sight, Peter and I were off to Restaurant Fukier for lunch. That's right, Fukier. And it's not misspelled.

Anyway, it was at this lunch that Peter offered to tell me the legend of Gonzo the Parrot as I stared at the colorful bird perched in its cage in the corner.

I asked Peter to begin the story with "Once upon a time," regretting that Undersecretary Doogie wasn't there to enjoy it.

It seems that on a cold wintery night in years past, four businessmen arrived from China. No, they were not Chinese. They were Americans, just coming from a big business deal in the former lair of the Red Menace. One was from California and the other three were from Minneapolis, a city just as cold as Warsaw. So, they felt at home. They met at the corner table at Fukier with a local lawyer who insisted he had all the connections necessary for any deal in Warsaw. The only problem was that the meeting was held next to Gonzo, who turned out to be a lawyer-hating Polish parrot. The more the ambulance chaser talked, the louder Gonzo chirped. The more the shyster droned on, the more the three from Minneapolis nodded off, deprived of sleep. So nothing ever came of that fateful meeting. The lawyer has never been seen since. And the businessmen from Minneapolis and California lived happily ever after. The moral of the story, I concluded, was when in the presence of a lawyer, "May the Parrot be with you." And then it hit me. The one from California was Peter and the three from Minneapolis were Eddie Phillips and two of his top executives. I was sitting in the very restaurant where the plans to launch Belvedere vodka were first hatched. It was a holy place. I could hardly hold back my tears at the heartfelt story and my love for Gonzo. He hated lawyers almost as much as I did.

So bravely, I got up from the table and approached Gonzo as the parrot stared at me from its perch. "Parrotski wants a crackerski?" I asked. Silence.

"You see, Peter," I said with glee, "Gonzo doesn't hate me and I'm a lawyer."

It was then that the waiter told me the restaurant had

Gonzo's vocal cords cut because he made too much noise ever since that night so long ago.

"Screw the bird," I concluded.

Day Six

Back at Paul's offices to work on papers.

The night before, Peter found time to watch the Discovery Channel's report on spies in the twentieth century. Not a good idea. He decided he needed to become a real spy to continue with our mission. That's all we need now, I said to myself. A guy who wants to impersonate James Bond.

The first thing Peter decided to do was buy a cellular phone. Unfortunately, in Poland buying a cell phone is like finding a heart donor, still alive, who is willing to give up his heart just for the hell of it. Talk about bureaucracy!

After two hours of searching, we made our way to some old, deteriorating Communist monolith built for Poland by Stalin. Again, lots of goons hanging around who looked like security but who don't do a damn thing. I realized that there really wasn't any security in Poland. Just a lot of people who looked like security. Faux security.

We ended up in some office where the local salesman came out with three boxes of cell phones, one green, one blue, and one black. The green and blue ones looked really stupid. The black one looked cool. So Peter chose the black one.

"Sorry," Mr. Phoneski said, "the black one is broken."

And you wonder why there are so many Polish jokes? This guy shows Peter a broken phone! So Peter took the green one because it reminded him of the color of one of the political parties in Poland. Why can't the political parties just have names, or would that be too hard to remember? I wondered.

Now you'd think that Mr. Phoneski might have a phone number to go along with the phone. Not. So Peter and I politely suggested to the idiot that maybe the phone wouldn't work so well without one. After some thought, Mr. Phoneski said he could get one if Peter gave him 1,100 zlotych, the currency of Poland. After already giving him a credit card, I wondered why he wanted some cold cash, too. But having now spent six days in Poland, even I didn't bother to ask. So I reached into my wallet and gave Peter most of my zlotych. Peter was short on cash. Paying really didn't bother me. After all, it was really stupid-looking money. Mr. Phoneski put it in his wallet, certainly intending to pay it to the phone company at the appropriate time.

So now Mr. Phoneski agrees he can get a number. Only problem is he doesn't know what it is but promises, if Peter keeps the phone off (that's right, "off"), that it will be beamed to the phone from outer space and magically appear on the display. On the display of the turned-off phone! Again, having been in Poland for six days, that sounded perfectly logical to me and off we went with Peter's new toy turned off waiting for the Polish space station to zap down a phone number. No question that it was time to get out.

Next Peter and I, with his new spy equipment, were whisked off to Zyrardow, a small berg west of Warsaw where Belvedere, the elixir so attractive to the dirty Frenchmen, was made. We had an appointment with the local prosecutor and were anxious as we approached the office.

Her door was locked, despite the fact that we had an appointment. Then she showed up in the hall from another office, unlocked the door, and showed us into her small, cramped office. I figured she was about thirty, although based on the quality of life evident in this town, she could have been thirteen or so and just looked like she was thirty.

While hearing our tale of woe, she nodded her head a lot. Kind of like those Bobblehead dolls on the back of old Chevys driven in Los Angeles. We were about to depend on some Bobblehead doll to investigate a multimillion-dollar case?

At the end of the conversation, Peter asked about personal safety in these cases.

"Oh," she said as her head bobbed up and down, "I live with threats every day. The last prosecutor had acid thrown in her face. And the one before that had his kids kidnapped. But that's not a problem for me. I don't have any family."

I understood her to mean that not only did we have a thirteen-year-old Bobblehead doll handling the case, she was also a lunatic ready for an instant face lift just because she had no one to go home to.

The trip back was uneventful and I bid farewell to Peter, as I knew I was leaving in the morning, escaping from Warsaw with the same volume of blood I arrived with. A good deal.

As I settled in my room, the door suddenly opened and two bruisers in red jumpsuits walked into the room. I just stared at them, my life passing by as I wondered why I made it so close to escape, only to fail.

"There's a problem with window. Can we fix?" said Red Giant Number One. Red Giant Number Two nodded. I was speechless, worrying more about whether I had an extra pair of underwear. So the two walked by and fixed the window. It was broken.

After they left, I went to bed and spent my last night in Warsaw dreaming of the freedom I would savor with the arrival of the next day's sunrise.

Day Seven

I couldn't get up early enough and managed to get to the airport with an hour to spare. I went through security, knowing that it didn't mean a damn thing anyway, and walked up to the ticket counter.

"You should have a pre-paid ticket for me," I said to the lady handling check-in.

"If you don't have a ticket, you need to go upstairs and get one first."

Undaunted and refusing to let anyone get between me and my escape, I made my way through the Warsaw airport and went upstairs to the British Airways ticket office.

The desk clerk looked up at me and said, "Oh, yes, sir. We've got your ticket ready. Just sign here."

How, I wondered, did they know who I was? Quickly remembering the futility of asking questions in Poland, I took the ticket, thanked him, and got my ass on the British Airways flight faster than I could say, "Get me the hell outta here."

You're in NATO Now

It wasn't long before I was back in Poland, this time in Szczecin, the home of Starka, a vodka flavored with linden and apple tree leaves that is aged in oak barrels. When bottled, it has the color of scotch and the taste of compost. But for some crazy Poles, it's a delicacy. And it was something my client, Eddie Phillips, wanted me—along with Peter, the consultant, and one of Eddie's right-hand men—to investigate and tie up with an exclusive licensing agreement. Eddie wanted to corner the compost vodka market!

As usual, what was supposed to be a routine trip to meet

with the distiller turned into yet another Phillips adventure.

If we drove from Warsaw to the distillery, it would take us at least eight hours if we were lucky and the roads not jammed. So Peter decided we'd fly to Szczecin. But Peter being Peter, why fly in a simple, conventional airplane? Nope. Peter arranged for us to take a Russian helicopter. It seems that since the end of the Cold War and the fall of the Soviet Union, there were a lot of spare helicopters in Warsaw, and some oligarchs posing as entrepreneurs were renting them out to fools like us who wanted to fly to Szczecin.

So off to the landing field we went. What greeted us was the largest helicopter I'd ever seen. It was a monster straight out of *Rambo*. Ominous.

The two pilots greeted us and we boarded. The rotors groaned and came to life. The noise was deafening.

My companion and I sat in the back; Peter sat closer to the pilots. We could see the dashboard with hundreds of lights and the cockpit windshield ahead. For the next two hours, we rocked and rolled our way to Szczecin. It was a miserable ride but at least we got there.

Our meetings ran late and it was past nine o'clock when we made our way back to our ride, the helicopter from hell. On the way, I suggested to Peter that maybe we should find another way to return to Warsaw.

"Nonsense. Helicopters are great. We'll be back in the bar at the Bristol in no time."

I exchanged a doubtful glance with my fellow passenger but knew we'd never change Peter's mind. He was a stubborn Pole indeed.

So once again the engines groaned, the rotors spun, the behemoth rose, and we headed east to Warsaw.

About an hour into the flight, the weather took a turn for the worse. It started to snow. Hard. So hard we could no longer see anything outside, including through the cockpit windshield. But, the two of us reasoned, we had nothing to worry about since the aircraft undoubtedly had the necessary radar or whatever it needed to take us safely to Warsaw and the now much-desired bar.

It was then that the lights on the dashboard flashed and all went out. This was followed by a frantic conversation in Polish between the two pilots. While neither I nor my companion in the adventure spoke a dime of Polish, it didn't take us more than a minute to know there might be a problem. A serious problem. I shouted, "Peter, what the fuck is going on?" I think the pilots heard me. They spoke frantically to Peter.

A pilot started pointing down. The other nodded "yes." So we landed. In someone's back yard. In the middle of Poland. They shut down the engines, and all was quiet.

One of the pilots opened the door and ventured out into the snowy night. We all followed. We were greeted by what we assumed was the family that lived in the house, and in whose yard we just landed. They were simply staring at us. I was convinced they looked upon us as alien beings from another planet that had landed their spaceship in their backyard.

The pilot started a conversation with the local owner when the police arrived. At that point, the discussions got noticeably more animated. Shouting. Arms waving. The pilots objecting. Peter trying to be calm. The two of us stood there, helpless and speechless. Speechless in Poland. If we could have run away, we would have. But the cops had guns, so we dismissed that idea quickly.

Finally, Peter returned and told us, "We have to get back

on the helicopter and fly it over to a local military base or they will arrest us for illegally landing a plane in someone's backyard. And trust me, we don't want to be arrested in this town."

I couldn't believe he suggested such a stupid idea. "Get back on the helicopter, Peter? Are you fucking crazy? It's broken, Peter. Why on earth would we willingly get back on a broken helicopter so we can try to fly it to some military encampment undoubtedly equipped with all sorts of things that can shoot us down?"

"It's that or we go to jail."

The proverbial Hobson's Choice.

We got back on the helicopter. Once again the engines groaned, the rotors spun, the behemoth rose, and we headed into the night in search of the secret military base. The only good news was that the snow had stopped and the lights on the dashboard were working again. We had hope, but not for long.

About fifteen minutes into our flight, the lights went out again and the helicopter started to shudder violently. It started to rock and roll. It started to drop like a rock. It was obvious we were about to crash. That jail cell we passed up started looking pretty good.

We hit the ground very hard and anything not bolted down flew. God only knows why He looked down on us with His grace, but we all seemed to be intact. A bit shaken up, but alive and free of any bleeding gashes.

"Holy shit," I said to my fellow traveler. "We just survived a fucking helicopter crash. Unbelievable." By the expression on his face, I concluded that while he shared my fright, he didn't share my amazement. And once we saw the pilots frantically trying to leave the helicopter with Peter in close pursuit, we decided it was time to leave, too. We jumped out and were greeted by a pool of mud and a quagmire. As we stepped forward, the suction from the mud took off our shoes. We were now in wet muddy ground in our socks.

As we stood there trying to assess the situation, we noticed that a convoy of military vehicles were fast approaching.

"Peter," I yelled, "please make sure you tell them that they're part of NATO now and our allies. They're not Russian communist sympathizers and we're not their enemies!" I guess I was a little upset. It was bad enough preferring to be in jail where I'd have shoes than on the wrong end of some trigger-happy soldier.

When the soldiers arrived and jumped out of their vehicles, weapons in hand, animated discussions followed. Thankfully, things calmed down and we were put in the back of a vehicle. We were taken to a cold building where Eddie's representative and I sat, wet feet and all, while Peter negotiated our release. By about 1:00 a.m., we were told we could leave.

"Leave?" I asked Peter. "And where the fuck are we supposed to go?"

"Warsaw," Peter responded.

"OK, Peter. And how are we going to get there? In case you haven't noticed, our ride is out there sinking in the mud."

"They called us a taxi."

"A taxi? We're going to take a fucking taxi back to Warsaw in the middle of the night? That's the plan?"

"Yep. Don't worry, we'll be fine." So off we went to get our taxi.

What arrived was a Lada, a Russian-built car adapted from a Fiat 124 sedan. I later learned that it was supposedly reengineered to deal with Russia's harsher climate and poor roads. Right. I was soon to learn that a Lada is constructed more with duct tape than rivets.

My companion and I got in the back seat. Peter rode shot-gun. Off we went down unlit and deserted roads in the middle of Poland. No one was talking.

Suddenly, the driver lost control of the car. Why? Because a fucking wheel fell off. On an unlit and deserted road in the middle of fucking Poland. We ground to a halt and tried to relax while the driver dug out his spare and started trying to put it on the Lada.

This is perfect, I thought. We avoided jail, survived a hel-icopter crash, lost our shoes in muck, and were spared a military firing squad only to find ourselves stranded in the middle of the night on an unlit and deserted road in the middle of fucking Poland with a car now left with three wheels. What more could go wrong?

That's when my buddy suggested I look at the other side of the road. Standing there, staring at us, was a wolf. I swear he was grinning and sizing us up for a midnight snack. And he was growling.

As we watched the wolf moved back into the woods, no doubt to get some reinforcements. We decided to get closer to the Lada.

Thankfully, we saw that the driver had attached the wheel and we wasted no time getting in and roaring off. It took four more hours, but at about 5:00 a.m. we arrived at the Bristol. I walked up to the desk clerk, muddy socks and all, and said with absolute conviction, "You're going to open the bar and we're going to have a drink and I don't want to hear any shit to the contrary."

Maybe it was the sheer laser beams that were emanating from my eyes that convinced him I was not going to take no for an answer. He made a call. They opened the bar. And we drank until dawn, shoeless.

But not all of our adventures were just in Poland.

Firing the Vice President of the United States

By 1998, things were really hot with the Belvedere bottle broker. We had suits with them in more than a dozen countries. Eddie Phillips was spending hundreds of thousands of dollars in legal fees. It was a mess and needed to stop.

To gain some leverage, the bottle broker hired a Washington lawyer who had a reputation as an international negotiator and a tough SOB. Knowing that "lawyer" and "SOB" were redundant, his reputation didn't impress me. Not so with Eddie. He called and told me he decided to retain Walter Mondale, the former vice president of the United States, to lead negotiations with the SOB. Eddie was told Mondale knew the SOB and would make easy work of him.

So we briefed Mondale.

It took him no time at all to screw it up. Eddie was furious.

"Now what do we do?" he asked.

"First, we fire Mondale. And then we hire someone else who is even better."

"Who?" asked Eddie.

"I don't know yet. I'll think about it. In the meantime, we're firing Mondale."

I remembered that I had a law school classmate who was a partner of former U.S. Senator George Mitchell of Maine. President Bill Clinton had asked Mitchell to lead the efforts to find peace in Northern Ireland. I reasoned that if he could find peace there, he could help us settle our case with the

French. So I reached out to my classmate for an introduction. Eddie and I interviewed Senator Mitchell and retained his assistance.

Senator Mitchell was a consummate gentleman and statesman. He dove into the case and immersed himself in the facts. His grasp of all the complications was astounding.

What ensued was one of the most amazing periods of my life.

We decided I'd go to Paris and lead the negotiations there, with Mitchell giving me advice as needed. It had to be that way because in 1998 Senator Mitchell's prime directive was the peace negotiations in Belfast, Ireland, a one-hour time zone behind Paris.

I worked on negotiations during the day and called Senator Mitchell in the evening for advice. The senator's advice was on target every time I asked, but that's not what I most remember about those days. Most memorable were the conversations I had with him about his negotiations in Belfast. Although of course he never revealed any confidential information, the mere fact that I was talking at night with an American legend doing an immeasurably important job was humbling, to say the least. One of my last conversations with him was on the day he sealed the deal for the Good Friday Agreement and brought the first prospect of true peace to Ireland.

With Senator Mitchell's help, we did eventually settle the differences with the bottle broker, but that paled in comparison to having the opportunity to work with one of the greatest statesmen the United States has ever known.

Birds over Cuba

In 2000, I got a call from Eddie Phillips. I always knew that when he called it was likely to be the beginning of yet another adventure.

"Doug, we're going to Cuba. I have it on high-placed authority that the United States is about to end the embargo and allow Cuban imports. I want to get to Havana now and corner rum exports."

Being a cigar smoker, I always wanted to go to Cuba but knew I couldn't under the embargo that President John F. Kennedy instituted after the Bay of Pigs fiasco in 1962.

"Eddie, not only do I seriously doubt the accuracy of your sources, but we can't go to Cuba. It's illegal and neither of us should be risking a violation of the Trading with the Enemy Act. Neither of us needs to go to prison for ten years."

"Can't we get around that? You're my lawyer, figure it out."

"Eddie, it's not worth the risk unless we have a special approval of the Treasury Department to be there for charitable or educational purposes."

Eddie said he'd call me back. The idea left my mind.

About a week or so later, Eddie called back.

"Doug, we're going to Cuba. I worked it out with the University of Minnesota to accompany a group that's going to Havana for a conference to study the migratory habits of birds. We'll go under their Treasury permit. So pack your bags."

"To study the migratory habits of birds, Eddie? Really?"

"Stop asking questions. Maybe we'll learn something about birds. You want to go to Cuba, don't you? And I need you there to help me negotiate the deal with the rum makers."

What could I say?

When we landed in Havana, the professor with the knowledge of birds asked us if we'd like to go to any of the seminars.

"No thanks," Eddie responded, "we'll see you in couple of days." So much for studying the migratory habits of birds. But I knew Eddie never planned to learn a fucking thing about the damn birds.

We checked into the Parque Central Hotel. It was a lot nicer than I expected. Pretty modern and overlooking Havana. The rooftop bar was terrific and the mojitos perfect. It took us no time to light cigars and enjoy the view, drinks in hand.

The next day, we were off to a cigar factory. Amazing experience. Just like I'd heard in myths, there was a person reading propaganda aloud as row upon row of rollers made cigars. It was a cigar lover's heaven. Of course, I bought one hundred cigars.

That night, we ate dinner at a *paladar*, a private home that is allowed to host tourists for an evening meal. We had chicken, rice, and of course, plenty of rum. And we smoked cigars. While the meal itself was decidedly mediocre, it didn't matter. We were relaxing on a warm night amid wonderful hospitality. It struck us that we felt completely safe in Havana as we walked all around the city, day and night.

Back at the Parque Central, I called my wife. My cell phone worked fine from the roof of the hotel.

"Are you OK?" she asked.

"Yes, why?"

"CNN is reporting that there are riots in Havana over the crap about Elián González. He's the kid Janet Reno is trying to throw out of the United States and send back to Cuba."

"Really? You could fool me. I'm on the roof of my hotel overlooking all of Havana and I don't see or hear a thing. Unless they're hiding them from plain view, I'm fine."

So there you have it. There was even fake news in 2000.

The next day, Eddie and I went to the distillery. They were very cordial. We sampled some great rum. Eddie looked at me with his, "OK, start negotiating" look.

"So, Señor, we'd like to talk to you about entering into a distribution contract for the U.S. market as soon as the embargo is lifted. We have had considerable success in distributing luxury spirits in the states and would like to do the same for you." Eddie smiled at me.

Señor didn't smile. His expression was more like, "Where the fuck did these two gringos come from?"

"Señor Phillips and Wood, we are flattered by your interest. But we currently have a contract that is controlled by the government and we cannot grant any rights to anyone without their approval." I think he really wanted to end the sentence with, "you two capitalist fools."

Undaunted, and knowing that Eddie would never take no for an answer, I bluffed on.

"Señor, we know that you are locked into a government contract. But we believe that will all change in the near future. So we'd like to discuss how the two of us can take advantage of the market when it opens up."

"I see. I suggest we then wait until it opens up. Then we'd be happy to discuss it with you."

"That would be fine, Señor." I knew we'd get nowhere.

They bid us farewell. They didn't give us a bottle for our efforts.

"Why did you give up so easily on getting the rights?" Eddie asked.

"Look, Eddie. The guy wasn't in any position to negotiate.

It was clear the government controls the rights and he was not about to screw with Fidel. And frankly, neither can we. Unless you missed it, cornering the rum market doesn't have a damn thing to do with the migratory habits of birds. We shouldn't even be discussing this shit with them."

"OK. OK. Calm down. Let's go to a bar."

Back in Havana, we walked through a park where a flea market was under way. There were quite a few flea markets, as the locals were doing their best to make a few extra bucks off tourists.

The prices were great, and I bought a nice painting.

As we walked, a beggar came up to us and asked for a quarter. Eddie, as he always did, reached into his pocket to help the man and gave him a dollar. We walked on. A few minutes later, the beggar showed up again. My first reaction was that here we go. The bum is going to try to hit Eddie up for more. Just as I was about to step in between Eddie and the beggar, the beggar extended his hand and offered Eddie three quarters in change and said, "Señor, I only asked for a quarter. Here is your change."

We were flabbergasted. Change from a beggar! This sure as hell wasn't the Cuba I expected.

After three days, it was time to leave. At the airport, the bird professor asked if we'd like to spend a few minutes with him to talk about the migratory habits of birds in case we were asked about it when we got to U.S. Customs.

"No thanks," responded Eddie. "We'll be fine."

Fine? I thought. How are we going to be fine if we're asked about fucking birds?

Our flight from Havana to Cancun was short, and Eddie and I split up there. He was flying into Chicago and I was going back to New York via Houston.

In Houston, I filled out the white immigration/customs form and declared my cigars and painting, listing Havana as one of my ports of call. When I handed it to the immigration officer, she said (or more like barked), "You can't go to Cuba. It's illegal."

"I went on a Treasury permit. So it's OK." I was starting to get nervous. Where was the damn bird professor when I needed him?

"Let me see it." I handed it to her. She looked at it for about five minutes and typed all sorts of things into her computer, no doubt trying to determine if I was a Cuban agent or wanted by Interpol.

Finally, she handed it back to me and said, "You go over there to the table and wait for the Customs officer."

Under a Treasury permit, you were allowed a maximum of one hundred dollars in non-exempt goods. And while my painting was exempt, my cigars were not.

After standing at the table for about five minutes and thinking that they're probably looking at me from behind two-way mirrors to examine telltale signs of a smuggler, the Customs officer appeared. He was the size of a fucking elephant, undoubtedly a middle linebacker for the Minnesota Vikings before he decided to protect our borders.

"Let me see your passport and permit."

I handed them to him. He took them and went back through the door from where he'd come, no doubt so he could further observe me as my sweat got worse the more I thought about the prospect of a full body search, cavities and all.

After what seemed like an eternity, he reappeared with another elephant officer at his side.

Jesus, I wondered, how much trouble am I in? Do I look

that dangerous? Do they have to give me any warnings before they arrest me and probe to their hearts' content?

Elephant 1 spoke. "Please empty your bag and show us all the goods you bought."

So I took out my cache of cigars, ten neatly packed in each of ten separate baggies, and began piling them on the table. It reminded me of the scene in *Close Encounters of the Third Kind.*

"So," Elephant 1 asked, "you paid a hundred dollars for all those cigars?"

"Yes," I responded. I thought confessing too soon was a bad tactic.

Elephant 2 spoke as he looked at my permit. "So, why don't you tell us something about the migratory habits of birds."

Fuck.

I figured I had three options. Lie and make something up. Tell the truth and throw myself at their mercy. Or try humor and see if making them laugh would get me off the hook— assuming anyone can make two elephants laugh.

My mind was in overdrive as I considered the options. I resolved that lying was not a good idea. It never is. So I rejected that option. Telling the truth, while attractive, wasn't all that appealing, given my desire to avoid the body search. So I settled on humor.

"Well," I responded, "to tell you the truth, they fly, shit, and then continue flying. Right over the island on their way to South America." I tried to look serious.

Both shook their heads, but I noticed a tiny little smile on Elephant 1 as he said, "Fine. Get out of here."

"Can I take my cigars?" I asked.

"Take your damn cigars and get out of here before we change our minds."

I've never looked at birds the same again.

Houston, We Have a Problem

It was the week before parent's day at my kid's summer camp outside Lake George, New York. My wife and I were looking forward to seeing them after four weeks apart. It was a command performance.

Then Eddie Phillips called.

"Doug, we have to go to Houston for a meeting with mucky-mucks from Poland. They're having some sort of Polish celebration or dinner, or something like that. But the who's who of Poland will be there and they'll be able to help us. I'm leaving tomorrow. Meet me there."

"Eddie, how long will we be there?" I cautiously asked.

"I don't know. Two or three days, I guess."

"I can't go, Eddie. It's parent's weekend at camp and there is simply no way I'm going to risk not being there. I can't."

"But I need you in Houston. I don't want to go without you."

I was flattered but unmoved.

"I understand, Eddie, but I can't. I hope you understand."

He was silent.

"Eddie, you OK?"

"Yeah. How about this. I'll charter you a private jet to bring you back so you won't have to miss a thing."

A private jet? Wow. I'd never been on a private jet.

"Are you sure I'd be back in time?" I could see what was coming but never wanted to miss an opportunity for another adventure with Eddie.

"I guarantee it. It will be fueled and ready at the airport

whenever you need it. And you can leave in plenty of time."

So I flew to Houston with a not-so-friendly goodbye from my wife, and a very clear, "You'd better be back in time" order.

I don't really remember much about the meetings. We met a bunch of Polish dignitaries, drank some vodka, and ate canapes. We schmoozed. And then it was Friday afternoon and time for me to go.

"Eddie, I have to leave for the airport now. I think we did well. I'll call you next week with what we need to do next to follow up, OK?"

"Sure. No problem. Thanks for making it. Have a good flight home and a good time at camp. Enjoy the jet."

Off I went to the airport, where I was greeted at the private hangar by a very nice young man. Behind him, just outside the hangar, sat a Gulfstream G550, popularly known as a G5, perhaps the most beautiful private jet in the world.

"Is that my plane?" I asked.

"Yes, it is. It's a beautiful aircraft."

"It sure is. When do we leave?"

"Well, that's the problem. You see, we're waiting for delivery of an organ for a transplant patient in New York. It's coming in from Mexico and we need to get it there as soon as it arrives. So I hope you don't mind waiting a little while."

An organ? For a transplant operation? And I need to wait? What else could I do?

"OK, I guess that will be fine as long as it's not too long. I can't afford to be late."

His expression wasn't exactly warm. "I'm sure you'll make it in plenty of time, Mr. Wood. We appreciate your understanding. Please have a seat."

So I sat. And sat. And sat. Watched the clock ticking away.

I asked if he had any word on where the organ was. He said he didn't. But he expected it to arrive any moment.

So I continued to sit. And sit. And sit. Watched the clock ticking away. I again asked if he had any word on where the organ was. He said he hadn't, but he expected it to arrive any moment.

Finally, I decided I could wait no longer. They'd have to find another jet for the organ. I was not going to miss parent's weekend. No way.

I went to the counter and demanded that we immediately leave. I could not wait any longer. It was my plane and I wanted to go. Now.

He was shocked but seemed suddenly compliant.

"Of course, Mr. Wood. I'll take care of it right away. I hope we can find another way to get the organ there on time."

Asshole attorney.

After about ten minutes, the desk agent said he had good news. They'd located another jet. Not for the organ. For me.

"What do you mean another jet? Why aren't I taking the G5? Is there another G5?"

"I'm sorry, Mr. Wood. But we absolutely have to keep this jet on hand for the organ. But don't worry, we have another jet being fueled right now and you can walk over to the hangar and get on board. You'll be in the air within an hour. You'll be in Teterboro airport in no time."

"Really?" I asked. "What kind of jet is it?"

He rattled off some name that I no longer remember. Suffice it to say there was no "G" or "5" in it.

When I arrived at the new hangar, what I saw was perhaps the smallest plane I'd ever seen. And it badly needed to be washed.

I was greeted by the pilot, a young man who looked as if

he'd just gotten out of bed. Great, I thought. My pilot is twelve years old and tired. Lovely.

"Hello Mr. Wood. We're just about ready. Let me show you to your seat."

What choice did I have?

The plane had only four passenger seats and virtually no headroom. You needed to bend over to get down the aisle.

"Mr. Wood, I suggest you go to the back of the plane and sit in the bench seat. It's bigger and more comfortable. You can stretch your legs out into the aisle. You'll also notice that one of the other seats has been removed and there is a wooden box with taps for vodka and scotch. There's an ice bucket and a glass. You can help yourself. I think we've got some nuts as well. I'll see if I can get you some."

Damn organ.

I crawled to the back of the plane, filled the glass with ice, and pulled the tap for vodka. He never did bring me any nuts.

But I made it to parent's weekend, hangover and all.

And then, of course, Eddie and I would always have Paris.

Jail and the Escape from France

If you ever want a lesson in how wonderful our judicial system is, try dealing with due process in France. There's a reason why they used to behead people in the city square. Just ask Marie Antoinette. While my client avoided the guillotine, irrational French justice got a little too close for comfort.

In 2001, while we were in the midst of our heated battles with the French bottle broker who supplied the Belvedere vodka bottles, they went public on the *Nouveau marché*, the French stock market for small issues, which was very popular with start-

ups and companies looking for quick financing. The bottle broker went public and, to put it mildly, made a killing. Problem
was that as far as my client was concerned, the promotional
materials grossly misrepresented their rights vis-à-vis Belvedere
vodka. So we hired a fancy local Paris lawyer and complained
to the market regulators. We had some nice meetings. And that
was it. They didn't care. After all, why should they listen to some
cowboy from the States attacking one of their always innocent
citizens?

Frustrated, we sought the advice of the local branch of an
international public relations agency.

"What can we do to expose these lies?" we asked.

"Launch a website and tell the truth," they advised.

"Can we do that?" we asked the fancy Paris lawyer.

"Yes. Just tell the truth."

And so the website was launched with meticulous care in
telling only the facts about who owned what and who had the
rights to Belvedere vodka. And it worked. Their stock prices fell
in the face of the truth.

Then we learned that unlike any reasonable and civilized
society, in France you can privately charge someone with a
crime. No need to investigate whether the charges are true. Just
file a frickin' criminal complaint.

No one—not the fancy Paris lawyer or the fancy public
relations agency—told us about that possibility.

When my client found itself criminally charged in Paris
for disrupting the life of the bottle broker with the website, we
were a bit surprised. And angry.

So we hired another fancy Paris lawyer. He told us that no
one had ever launched such a website in France. It was unprece-
dented. My reaction? I thought it would have been nice if the

first set of fancy Paris lawyers had told us that. Or maybe the fancy Paris public relations agency that developed the website could have told us that. I guess it never occurred to them.

During the criminal investigation of the circumstances surrounding the controversy between the bottle broker and my client, Paris authorities requested that Eddie Phillips answer some questions in person. We were promised it was just a routine matter. It would just take an hour or so. Eddie agreed, and he and I, together with our new fancy Paris lawyer, showed up at the police station for the appointment.

We were greeted by a crusty cop who asked Eddie to follow him through a turnstile. Eddie did so. When I tried to follow, I was stopped.

"No. Sorry. You can't come in. Only Mr. Phillips."

I looked at our new Paris lawyer and said, "What's going on here? Why can't I stay with my client?"

Our fancy Paris attorney started an argument with the crusty cop. Many heated words, none of which I understood. After about ten minutes of screaming, our lawyer told me we should step outside so he could explain. Eddie was out of sight, having been taken down to some room somewhere for his inquisition.

Outside, I was informed by our fancy Paris lawyer that Eddie was going to be detained for much longer than an hour.

"What are you talking about?" I demanded. "We had a deal. The questioning was supposed to be for an hour. Now you're telling me Eddie's under arrest?"

"Well, not exactly. You see, here in France the police can detain someone for three days for whatever reason they feel like until they have to charge them with something. So they've decided to hold on to Eddie for now."

I blew my stack and started screaming at the lawyer, letting him know in no uncertain terms how I considered him responsible for this screwup that now meant my client was stuck in some dirty Paris jail for the next three days.

Amid my screaming, the crusty cop came out. I told our lawyer to ask the bastard what was going on and demand that Eddie be released.

Our Paris lawyer suggested I calm down.

Calm down? I thought. My fucking client is probably being tortured into a confession as we stood there and I'm supposed to calm down!

So the cop said, "We are detaining Mr. Phillips. Perhaps you would like to be detained, too."

Fuck, I thought, the bastard spoke English. He had heard everything I said about him.

Talk about losing my bravado in a split second. I loved Eddie and wanted to protect him. But there was no way I was also going to be retained and tortured on the rack. Screw that. I calmed down, and our lawyer suggested we leave.

Back at our fancy Paris lawyer's office, we mapped out plans on how to get Eddie out of jail and even better yet, out of France.

We called the America Embassy and I complained to the attaché, knowing full well that doing so was a waste of time. But doing anything made me feel better.

As we sat plotting how to free Eddie, the lawyer took a call. I could see from his face that he was not pleased. He hung up.

"We have to get you out of France. They're now looking for you, too."

Looking for me! They're looking for me! Who the fuck is looking for me?

"They want to question you. I don't want you detained."

The crusty cop was really getting on my nerves. So was the Paris lawyer.

"Fine, I'll go to Orly and catch the next flight."

"No. They'll be watching the airport. That is what they'd expect you to do. We'll take you to the train and you can take the Eurostar to London. One leaves in an hour. You'll have just enough time to get your luggage. Let's go!"

Once on the train, I called Eddie's right-hand man to give him an update. I ended the conversation with instructions to get a jet ready at Orly to fly Eddie out of France the moment he was released. I hung up and looked up. Everyone in the car was staring at me. I guessed I had been speaking loudly and they all heard about the guy who was arrested in Paris and for whom I was fueling a private jet so it would be ready to execute his escape. All I could do was smile.

Once in London, I checked into a hotel. It was too late to call home, so I went to the bar for a drink.

My phone rang. It was our fancy Paris lawyer.

"I have good news. We know were Eddie is. They moved him to a cell at an old prison here in Paris. He's scheduled for a hearing tomorrow. We need you to come back."

"Come back? Seriously? You told me a few hours ago that they were looking for me and now you want me to come back. What for? To face a firing squad? You think I'm nuts?"

"You'll be fine. Don't worry."

"Don't worry? You're the one who told Eddie he didn't have to worry. Now look where he is."

"It's important. We may need your testimony."

I had no choice. Back into the belly of the beast.

There was no immediate hearing. Instead, Eddie was

released and told to come back in a couple of days. They kept his passport. So we stayed in Paris and enjoyed the city. As was always the case with Eddie, he never showed an inkling of fear or concern. He took it all in stride. Inspiring as ever.

Hey, It's Just Money

And as for my fees and the decision to forgo 25 cents a bottle? Perhaps the dumbest decision I ever made in my life. Belvedere vodka was an astronomical success. Eddie sold millions of bottles, recouped his entire investment in less than two years, and ten years after the launch sold the brand to LVMH for more than $600 million. I stopped calculating what could have been to avoid depression!

I think Eddie felt a wee bit bad about my lack of faith in his business prowess. He took pity. After the closing with LVMH, he took me out to celebrate. When dinner was over, he handed me a check for one million dollars, telling me he wanted to be sure I personally profited from the sale, as had so many others who stood by his side over the years.

Imagine how I felt looking at a check made out to me for a million dollars! My head was spinning with all the things I could do with a million dollars. Buy a Maserati. Pay off my mortgage. Take a really great vacation.

"Eddie," I said after taking a deep swallow, "I am really flattered, but I can't take the money. If you want to give us a bonus, it has to go to the firm, not to me."

"Are you crazy? I don't want to give it to your firm. I paid them one hundred percent of their fees. They earned millions and I was happy to pay it. But I want you rewarded. Not them."

"I appreciate that and I think there are some folks at the

firm who have earned a bonus for the wonderful work they've done for you. But not me."

"OK, I want you to sleep on it. I want to do this for you. You need to make it happen."

We parted that night with hugs and I muddled about it over the next few days. A big part of me wanted to take the money. I suppose I could have found a way to hide it from the firm, but that was not something I was willing to do no matter how much I was offered. Some friends told me I was nuts.

"Take the money, you fool," they'd say.

"Stick it in the Cayman Islands as a retirement slush fund," another advised.

And I'd be lying if I said I didn't consider that advice. But I knew I could not. So I called Eddie with a compromise.

"Eddie, I really appreciate that you want to give me the money, but I simply can't take it. Instead, what I'd like you to do is give $250,000 to my firm with instructions that you'd like to see the team that worked with me rewarded from those funds. But I want you to tell the firm that I am not to be included. Whatever the firm decides to pay me cannot be tied to your payment. I'd like you to split the other $750,000 between three charitable organizations: $50,000 to my church, $50,000 to the Global Advertising Lawyers Alliance, and $650,000 to the Franklin Pierce Law Center."

"Are you sure?" Eddie pressed.

"Yes, I'm sure."

So I was a million dollars poorer than I could have been but at least in that one moment, I wasn't an asshole attorney. That felt good then and still feels good to this day.

the rest of
the story

chapter 25
Break a Leg

In 2003, I took over the job of chief negotiator for the advertising industry in its collective bargaining agreements with the Screen Actors Guild and the American Federation of Television and Radio Artists for actors who appear in television and radio commercials. With a price tag of over $3 billion, it's one of the largest collective bargaining agreements in the world and the largest in the entertainment industry; larger than the union agreements for television or motion pictures. That makes sense when you think about it. A lot more actors appear in commercials than in TV shows or movies. And commercials run a lot more times. So the residuals mount up. It pays to be a working actor in commercials.

The negotiations are held in New York every three years at a hotel picked by the unions. It has to be a union hotel, so they're sometimes not exactly the Peninsula or Ritz Carlton. But they're clean. We negotiate for six weeks. Six weeks in the hotel.

These negotiations get a little testy at times.

I remember three things that taught me how different actors are from assembly line workers. Actors are artists. They have a craft few can do. And they're always worried about their next gig, forever paranoid that their last one is, well, their last one.

In my first negotiations, I felt sorry for the extras. I believed they didn't get as much as they should. And I was representing management! I wasn't supposed to have compassion for the worker. But I did.

So I made a proposal that was favorable to them, thinking that my largesse would pay off with a concession in another area. My philosophy was to give a little to get a little.

During a break, an extra came up to me.

"Doug, I'd like to personally thank you for the offer you made."

Aha, I thought, my strategy is working. They'll be putty in my hands.

"But I'd like you to withdraw the offer. We don't want it."

"You don't want it?" I was incredulous. "The offer is good for you. You'll make more money."

"Maybe, but we'll also anger the principal performers." Principal performers are the actors with speaking roles or who are prominently featured in a commercial.

It was later explained to me that no one wanted to anger the principals, not necessarily because they were revered or feared, but because every extra believed that he or she will one day be a principal and cash in. Never mind that the likelihood of that happening is remote; it does happen. And therein lies the amazing thing about actors. They're dreamers who never lose their dreams. They work as waiters and waitresses, taxi drivers, maids, handymen, and whatever else they need to do to make enough for a meal. But they never stop believing that their next audition is their first step to stardom and the Hollywood dream.

You have to respect that.

Another year, I was standing in the hallway. A reasonably well-known tough guy character actor walked up to me.

"Doug, may I have a word with you?"

No doubt he wanted to complain about something I'd said during negotiations.

"Of course. I love your work." I thought that would soften him up.

He maneuvered the two of us to a corner.

"I just want to tell you that in the old days, if someone made an offer like you just did, we would have taken him out back and broken his knees."

I felt the knot in my stomach.

"Well," I responded, "please tell me if you really mean that or if you're acting. Because if you are acting, you're doing a very good job. And if you're not acting, then we have to call the police."

He stared at me and said, "You'll never know." He walked away.

I never saw him at negotiations again. Too bad. He was a very good actor.

But the most exciting moment for me was at the Warwick Hotel at 2:00 a.m. We'd been negotiating all night and didn't adjourn until after midnight. I couldn't sleep, so I went downstairs to go for a walk.

As I crossed the lobby, a voice from the couch called out, "Hi Doug."

I didn't recognize him.

"Hi. I'm afraid you have the advantage. I don't recognize you."

"I'm here with SAG."

I walked over to him and sat down. "Oh, you're an actor. Tell me what you've done."

"Well you probably know me most as the voice of Bullwinkle Moose."

"Get out! I loved Bullwinkle. You have to lay some Bullwinkle on me."

And he did. And he was great. We talked about the series and all the fun he had portraying the big lunkhead. I loved it. I had a conversation with Bullwinkle J. Moose!

It doesn't get better than that.

chapter 26
Freebies

When I was a young attorney at Hall Dickler, my mentor, Felix Kent, told me how he and his wife had just spent a few days at a resort attending a meeting with our client, a group of independent ad agencies. He gave them an update on legal issues, hobnobbed with the agency owners, and had a great time. Better yet, the network paid all the expenses for both Felix and his wife.

I got to thinking what a great freebie that was for Felix and how I'd like to get a few of those kinds of gigs, too. I could couple networking and business development with a great time. What could possibly be better?

I did a little research and identified six other independent agency networks. I also noted there were associations like the American Association of Advertising Agencies (4A's), the Association of National Advertisers (ANA), the American Advertising Federation (AAF), the Western States Advertising Association, the International Advertising Association (IAA), and the World Federation of Advertisers (WFA).

While I knew about the 4As, ANA, and AAF, I didn't know much about the independent networks. So, I wrote letters to each of the networks offering to give a free yearly update at their annual meetings, provided they paid us a nominal retainer and covered the expenses for me and my spouse to the fete.

Eventually, five of them bought the deal. The deal I made with the sixth was different, since they didn't have annual meetings.

It proved the old adage: If you want it, you have to ask for it.

I must have done something right. Much to my surprise, my talks became big hits, and trips soared. Over the decades that followed, these wonderful networks brought me and my wife to fantastic venues, including Hawaii, Acapulco, Brussels, Paris, St. Martin, Captiva, London, Scotland, Ireland, Amsterdam, Orlando, Palm Springs, Miami, Ft. Lauderdale, Palm Beach, Key West, New Orleans, Coeur d'Alene, Washington, Atlanta, Chicago, and more. As my reputation grew, other associations brought me, all expenses paid, to exotic locations such as St. Petersburg, Beijing, South Korea, Shanghai, Singapore, Toronto, Stockholm, and more.

The most memorable freebie, however, is Dubai, where another lawyer and I were asked to give an hour talk at an advertising festival on advertising law developments in self-regulation. Yawn.

They offered us round-trip first-class travel on Emirates airline, five nights in the Fairmount hotel (inclusive of all meals in the hotel), a driver for the days we were there, and $10,000. All that to hear us talk for an hour.

On the day of our presentation, the two of us waited patiently backstage. We were the last speakers of the day. Immediately before us, an ad executive from Pakistan was talking about some topic I can't remember. Probably because it wasn't memorable. He went over his time limit. Way over. The organizers did nothing to speed him along or give him the hook. And he was so boring that people started leaving.

When he finally shut up, the host told us, "I'm so sorry,

but you only have ten minutes. Can you do your presentation in ten minutes?"

As if two lawyers could ever do anything in ten minutes!

But being the troopers we were and realizing most everyone had already left anyway, we said sure.

We introduced ourselves, delivered about five minutes' worth of comments on self-regulation, and wished everyone a nice life.

Ten minutes. Ten thousand dollars. One thousand dollars a minute. The equivalent of sixty thousand dollars an hour.

If there is a listing in *Guinness World Records* for collecting freebies, I'm in the running for it.

chapter 27
Giving Thanks

For years, like most other business people, I mailed holiday cards to clients. After all, I received enough of them and comfortably fell into the routine just like everyone else. Then I read *Swim with the Sharks Without Being Eaten Alive* by Harvey B. Mackay. It's a book, together with Dr. Norman Vincent Peale's *The Power of Positive Thinking* and Niccolo Machiavelli's *The Prince*, that I recommend to anyone in business.

Mackay's message is that successful businessmen need to break out of the clutter. They need to appeal to a client's personality as much as to their pocketbooks. And never, never get embroiled in politics or religion with clients. It occurred to me that while holiday cards were nice, they violated a number of Mackay's rules. They were ambiguous—were they religious or not, with "Holiday" vs. "Christmas" messages?

The only holiday that didn't violate the rules was Thanksgiving. It was nondenominational and celebrated giving thanks to everyone for all the good they do and the gifts we have. Yet I'd never received a Thanksgiving card from a client or business associate. So I decided to break the holiday card obsession and send thank-you notes to clients and friends at Thanksgiving. It broke through the clutter of December holiday cards and would offend no one. Or at least no one who had a heart and a brain.

But I wanted the cards to be more than a passing memory

that finds its way quickly into the trashcan at someone's desk. To that end, I decided to include with the card a CD of music I liked from lesser-known performers. Over the years, I sent CDs with performances by tenor Mario Frangoulis, Canadian country music singer Lisa Hewitt, saxophonist Mindi Abair, and James Belushi and The Sacred Hearts Band. In the year I toured through blues country in Tennessee, I sent a blues album with performances by T-Model Ford, Robert Balfour, and James Cotton. After a visit to Buenos Aries, I sent a CD of tango tunes. In the years I skipped the CD, I made contributions to charities, including Wounded Warriors, the Red Cross, and America's VetDogs. The greeting and sentiments in the card have always been well received and appreciated.

But it was what I did for two of those Thanksgivings that most reminded me why I should be the thankful one.

In 2010, I was trying to decide what CD to send with the card. I'd pretty much exhausted anything new and I didn't want to send something that was predictable or well known. My assistant, Nancy Schulein, mentioned to me that Ted (known as Theo or The-O) Getzoff was quite a singer, and he also played all sorts of musical instruments. While Nancy acknowledged that those talents were not that unusual, Theo also has autism. His father, Steve, who has Asperger's syndrome, had worked for me for more than a decade. He was a terrific and loyal employee, always willing to work the extra hour.

Nancy had me listen to a recording, and she was right. Theo was terrific.

Next Steve and Theo met with Nancy and me. Theo is a great talent, excited to sing and to learn new instruments. When I met him, he already played guitar, piano, and flute, all self-learned. He later went on to master more instruments.

Nancy and I decided to produce a CD of Theo's performances, calling it *My Irish Journey*. We became record producers!

The first CD had songs with an Irish theme. The jacket design and liner notes told Theo's story. It was inspiring then and still is today. Here's what I wrote to clients and friends:

As most of you know, for many Thanksgivings I have shared with my friends and clients music which has moved me over the past year and reminded me of how thankful we all should be for the blessings we have. But this year, it is very special.

I am proud to give you the music of The-O, a young man who is the son of my colleague Steve Getzoff. Ted Getzoff, aka The-O, is severely autistic. He only began to talk when he was five years old. Over the years of dealing with his challenges, The-O found music. In it, he found his voice and his confidence. His ability to learn instruments, arrange music, and perform is truly astounding. When Steve shared a rough demo with me and my assistant, Nancy Schulein, we knew immediately what we wanted to do this year—become record producers and share the wonder of The-O with all of you. So we put The-O in a studio and his first CD, *My Irish Journey*, was born!

Ted's story of success is made more inspiring when one realizes that his father, Steve, is afflicted with Asperger's syndrome, an autistic disorder. I learned of Steve's condition only after I hired him in 1997. Ever since, he never ceases to amaze me. Steve, like his son, has himself become a great success and is regarded in the IP world as one of the top trademark experts, teaching IP for the International Trademark Association and New York University School of Law, among others. He and Ted are true inspirations for all of us.

So as I say every year, find some time to get away from the headlines and television talking heads, sit comfortably and listen to music that I hope helps to clear your head, warm your heart and put life in perspective.

Happy Thanksgiving!

The response from clients and friends was overwhelming. They loved it. More important, the inspiration Theo instilled in everyone who listened to his performances was worth every second or dollar I spent producing the album.

Four years later, Nancy and I produced a second CD of Theo's performances—*My Sentimental Journey*. This time we featured opera, a talent Theo had developed over the years that is astounding. The CD was another great hit with clients and friends.

Thanksgiving remains my favorite holiday, and gives me the opportunity to express my thanks for all the blessings my family and I have received over the year. But out of all the things for which I give thanks every year, it is the gift that Theo, Steve, and their entire family have brought to me that is priceless.

You can find Theo on YouTube. Just search "The-O Get-zoff." You'll be amazed and, perhaps, thankful as well for your blessings.

chapter 28
Five Minutes with Arnold Schwarzenegger

One day in the late '90s I was sitting in my office going over the accounts receivables due the firm. We were in the middle of the year-end collections push and I was trying to get a handle on how well we'd do that year.

As I reviewed the computer sheets, I noticed an entry for M. Shanken Communications, publishers of *Wine Spectator* and *Cigar Aficionado*. As a cigar smoker, my curiosity was piqued and I called the lawyer who handled the client. Marvin Shanken, the owner of the publications, was (and still is) a legend in the wine and cigar industries.

"Sam, what do we do for Marvin Shanken?"

"Just general stuff."

"I want to meet him and pitch him for the work I do," I said.

"Why?"

"Why? Because I love cigars. Do I need any other reason?"

"I'll see what I can do."

Weeks passed before I received a call late one morning from Sam.

"I spoke to Marvin," Sam said. "He'll see you at 2:00 today. We have 45 minutes."

"Today?" I responded. "That gives me no time to prepare

the pitch. Can we make the appointment tomorrow or later in the week?"

"No. That's the time we have. You'll have to do the best you can."

I was in a small panic. No doubt I could bullshit my way through a pitch, but I had no idea what Marvin was like. I didn't know how to best approach him. But I was not about to pass up the opportunity.

At 2:00 Sam and I showed up for our appointment. It was the first time I'd been in the company's offices. In the center of the reception area was a glass-encased wine cellar with some of the rarest wines in the world. On the walls were original works of art no doubt worth a pretty penny. It was very elegant.

When I was brought in to see Marvin, he was sitting behind his desk—about the size of a Cadillac—smoking a cigar. After introductions, I went into my pitch about how wonderful we were and how much I appreciated the opportunity to present our abilities. Blah. Blah. Blah.

When I concluded, Marvin paused for a minute or so and said, "Thank you for coming by. But to be honest, I'm disappointed."

I was devastated. No one had ever told me they were "disappointed" with my canned pitch. They might not hire me, but they never expressed rejection in that manner.

I had to ask, "I'm confused. Why are you disappointed?"

In what I came to learn was Marvin's wry sense of humor, he responded, "Well, I give you the opportunity to pitch your business after Sam called me and you have no gift of appreciation for me." He gave me a deadpan look.

OK, I told myself. I can take this in two directions: One would be to apologize and get my ass back to my office.

The other was to fight fire with fire.

I looked Marvin straight in the eye and said, "To be honest, you gave me virtually no notice before I had to be here and I think I did pretty well given what little time you gave me. In truth, I'd say you owe *me* a gift of appreciation."

I held my breath. Marvin smiled, stood up, and told me to follow him.

He took me into his private walk-in humidor. It contained well over a thousand cigars. He reached for a Cuban Cohiba Siglo VI, one of the finest cigars in the world. Showing it to me, he asked, "So do you like Cohibas?"

I answered, "Yes. I love them."

"Good," he responded with a sly smile, "but you haven't earned this one yet." He put the Cohiba back on the shelf and picked some nondescript cigar that to this day I don't remember. "Here, you can have one of these. That's all you've earned for today. We'll see if you do better as we get to know one another."

That was the beginning of a wonderful relationship with a person who is not only a very successful businessman but also a very generous person who gives back in innumerable ways.

One of his favorite causes is the Prostate Cancer Foundation. He does an annual dinner that includes an auction of wines, cigars, vacations, and more that raises millions for research. Over the many years he's held the affair, more than $30 million has been raised to find a cure for prostate cancer. It's a star-studded event I don't miss.

In 2006, Marvin came up to me during the cocktail hour.

"Doug, we're auctioning off a humidor signed by Governor Arnold Schwarzenegger. Unfortunately he couldn't be here tonight, but I'd like you to start the bidding."

"Marvin, I don't need another humidor. I already have

more than I can use, including the one in my office that holds hundreds of cigars."

"I know that. I just want you to start the bidding. It's going to go for a pretty high price so you can just drop out of the bidding whenever you'd like."

"OK, Marvin. Whatever you need. I'm happy to do so."

After dinner, the auction began and got to the governor's humidor. After describing it, Marvin announced, "Let's open the bidding at $14,000." He looked at me.

My first thought was, Is he nuts? $14,000? And I have to start the bidding?

No one was taking the bait. He kept looking at me. I raised my hand.

Marvin said, "Thank you from my great lawyer."

No one else bid. The humidor was mine.

The guests at my table thought it was hilarious. I was "stuck" with a humidor I didn't need at a price I hardly expected to pay. But I had to make the best of it.

"Hey, it's not that bad," I told those gathered with me at the table. "It's a pretty big humidor so it must have at least twenty-five or more cigars in it. So I may have paid a lot for the humidor but no doubt I got plenty of cigars for it."

They brought over the humidor so my tablemates and I could admire it. It contained ten cigars. I paid $1,400 per cigar!

The table went wild. They're probably still laughing about it to this day.

A year passed, and I was once again at the annual dinner. So was Governor Schwarzenegger. During drinks at the tables, Marvin brought over the governor.

"Governor, I'd like you to meet Doug Wood, my lawyer and the person who bought your humidor last year."

We shook hands and the governor was very gracious. Marvin called to someone to find the photographer to get a picture of the three of us.

I interjected, "Marvin, we don't need any photo. I'm sure the governor has a lot of people to meet tonight and I don't want to get in the way or delay him."

Marvin looked a bit surprised, said OK, and the two moved on.

Later that night, Marvin asked me why I declined having a picture with the governor. After all, he told me, the photo would be in *Cigar Aficionado* and I'd have a few seconds of fame.

"The magazine comes to my house," I told him. "If my wife ever saw that I paid $14,000 for a humidor, signed or not signed by the governor, I'd be a soprano."

He laughed.

I wonder if Carol Ann will laugh now that I've confessed!

chapter 29
Daddy's Girls

On August 5, 2017, my daughter Andrea married Scott in a beautiful wedding at the Raphael Winery on the North Fork of Long Island. She is the first of my daughters to marry. I'll keep her age confidential but let's just say I'd been worrying about that day for decades. While I could not have been prouder of her and her new husband, letting go, as much of a cliché as that is, nonetheless haunted me. So I wanted to make sure my speech was a memorable and poignant one. I'd heard far too many speeches about how happy the family was, how much they loved the new spouse, how much they wished them the best, blah, blah, blah. I was committed to make mine different. It was also an interdenominational wedding. Andrea is Lutheran; Scott is Jewish. So I needed to be sensitive and careful not to offend anyone.

I also remembered words of wisdom my son, Joshua, unwittingly gave me when he was only ten. I was driving Josh and Meghan to some event. Josh was in the front seat; Meghan in the back seat.

Meghan broke the silence of the ride and asked, "Daddy?" in that tone that meant she wanted something I'd probably be inclined to say no to or tell her to go ask her mother.

Before I could respond, Josh said, "Dad, you're screwed."

To this day, I don't recall what Meghan asked for. No

doubt she got it. But I did learn that the most powerful word in the English language (and probably all others) is a question from a daughter that begins with "Daddy?"

I also had in mind all the less than memorable weddings I'd gone to, and wanted to make sure Andrea's was not one of them.

Her brother's wedding was anything but forgettable.

When Joshua married Bianca, the minister had a diabetic attack in the middle of the ceremony and nearly passed out. After someone helped him to the corner so he could sit down, Josh picked up the wedding book and continued with the ceremony, asking Bianca for her vows and reciting his own. Then he gave an ad lib soliloquy about how much he loved Bianca and what she meant to him. There wasn't a dry eye in the room. When he got to the "I now pronounce you husband and wife" part, he paused and said to the congregation, "I don't think I'm allowed to do this part." By then, the minister had enough wits about him to stand and recite the final words. They were officially married in a ceremony no one will ever forget.

And as if that were not enough, when Josh's newly minted father-in-law, Bill, went far too long in his speech, Josh rose and gave him the hook! To this day, no one who witnessed it has forgotten it. So the pressure was on. And I wanted to make sure I didn't get the hook from Scott.

Here's what I said (together with my "notes" on what to do during the speech):

> First and foremost, I'd like to thank you all for coming today to celebrate with Andrea and Scott. Having so many joining us is a gift we will never forget. And for those who could not join us today, I

know Andrea and Scott, and all of us, remember them in our hearts and thank them for the wonderful blessings they given us all.

As some of you know, I do a good deal of public speaking, at times before thousands of people. Over the years, I've gotten to a point where I'm no longer nervous when I stand in front of an audience.

But tonight is not about imparting boring legal advice on some boring topic. Tonight is about my daughter, Andrea, and the newest addition to our family, Scott. So tonight, I'm nervous and I ask that you bear with me if I stumble.

But there is one thing I've learned. To win over a crowd, always start with humor.

So I've got this great joke. Been thinking about it for more than a year. You're going to love it.

So a rabbi, a minister, and an aardvark walk into a bar . . .

[pause]

[look at Andrea and Scott]

Hmmm, now that I think about it, maybe that's not such a good joke after all. But that's OK, I've got another one I know you're going to love.

So a moyle, a pastry chef, and a snake walk into a bar . . .

[pause]

[let audience react]

[look at Andrea and Scott]

Maybe that's not a good one either.

So I'll move on.

As the father of the bride, tradition dictates that

I say something nice about Andrea and Scott. Some clichés about how we loved Scott when we first met him, how they're a perfect couple and "complete" one another. Yadda, yadda, yadda.

I'm going to dispense with that. The best man and maid of honor can cover it. Instead, I decided I'd tell you one story about Scott and Andrea that makes this day so joyous for Carol Ann and me.

Pretty early in their relationship, Scott visited us for a weekend. At the time, we really didn't know much about him. As a father, my first inclination was to be as suspicious as I was with anyone who dated my daughters. I figured I knew what Scott and every other boy wants. Hey, I even wrote a book about it. But unlike every other boyfriend Andrea ever brought home, when Scott arrived, he had a gift for Carol Ann. It was either candy or flowers. Doesn't really matter what it was. Nor was the gift the reason we opened our arms and hearts to Scott and knew Andrea had found a keeper. That happened a few days later after Scott had gone home. Our revelation came when Carol Ann got a handwritten thank-you card from him. Handwritten. I remember Carol Ann saying, "Hey, this kid was brought up right." And he was. So thank you Susan and Shelly for giving us such a wonderful son-in-law and Andrea a terrific husband.

OK. So much for the stories.

Another thing the father of the bride is supposed to do is bestow some words of wisdom on the bride and groom as they venture forth in their lives. After all, Carol Ann and I will celebrate our forty-fourth anniversary in twenty days. So I've certainly heard a lot of advice from Carol Ann over those years that I could use tonight. But now that I have to chance to give my own advice, I can't resist.

It's really simple.

I want to talk about F-words.

[to audience] Now, now. Don't get excited.

[to Andrea and Scott]

Given this crowd, it's probably best that I just talk to the two of you about a few f-words you should always focus upon.

Faith. Never lose your faith in God, your dreams, and in one another. Have faith in each other even when you think an idea is insane. Scott, knowing Andrea, I'm sure you've already heard a lot of ideas that may seem totally off the wall. And no doubt, she's heard a few zingers from you, too. Never let it be said that either one of you is lacking in dreams. But it is your dreams that bring a future filled with excitement and discovery. Always have faith.

Family. Family is the fabric that brings us all here today. Without family—including all our crazy aunts and uncles and annoying siblings, nephews, nieces, and cousins—we'd have no souls. We'd have no home. So no matter how frustrating family may sometimes be, never forget that it is your family that molded you into the two people who became one today.

[to audience] See folks, f-words don't have to be four letters.

[to Andrea and Scott] Now back to the words of wisdom and the next f-word.

Friends. Friends are the people who get you through tough times and help you celebrate the good ones. And while I've heard that some of your celebrations might at times go a little overboard, that's OK. Nor am I surprised. After all, the two of you and many of your friends went to the "U." And over-the-top celebrating comes with Miami's soul. Bottom line: Never forget that friends are forever.

And of course, let's never forget the last f-word I'd like to talk about. The f-word with four letters.

[to audience] OK, enough with the grunts and groans. We are all adults here and we can have a mature discussion about anything. Right?

And that last four-letter f-word is . . .

[pause]

Fate. The Greeks believed that on the day you're born, your fate and destiny is bestowed upon you by the Moirae, three goddesses who spun the thread of life, apportioned the fortunes that lay ahead, and decided when those fortunes would end. But I believe fate is in your hands. Never fear the future. Embrace whatever it brings. As my mom always said, "Never worry. Whatever may happen to you is for a good reason and will work out." For those of you who knew my mom, those are truly inspiring words.

So there you have it. F-words filled with wisdom. Or at least I think they are.

Now the last thing the father of the bride is supposed to do . . .

[pause]

[to audience] Yeah, yeah, yeah. I know what

you're thinking. Just shut up and sit down. And I will. But not before I give the toast.

So if you'll all please stand and raise your glasses.

To Andrea and Scott: May faith, family, and friends forever favor your future with times that are fun, fights that are few, hearts that are forgiving, faults that are forgotten, and the blessing that whatever fate may bring you, it is filled with fortunes and free of fears.

At Thanksgiving, Brent, my daughter Meghan's boyfriend of many years, asked for my blessing to marry her.

So now I've got another speech to worry about. The pressure I'm already feeling reminds me of another "f-word" often used to describe lawyers.

chapter 30
We Love to Hate Lawyers

How many lawyer jokes do you know? No doubt plenty. But as a lawyer, I bet I've heard them all. And they're never nice. Yet no one wants to say, "Hey, stop telling lawyer jokes. It's mean and spiteful. Lawyers are good people, and they have feelings, too. Be nice to them."

So you probably think I'm offended by lawyer jokes and insults constantly lampooning attorneys. As my friend from South Carolina said, "It's asshole attorney or fuckin' lawyer."

Surprise.

I hate lawyers, too. And I think lawyer jokes are hilarious.

Q: What's the problem with lawyer jokes?
A: Lawyers don't think they're funny, and no one else thinks they're jokes.

Q: What's the difference between a porcupine and a Mercedes-Benz full of lawyers?
A: The porcupine has pricks on the outside.

Q: If you are stranded on a desert island with Adolf Hitler, Attila the Hun, and a lawyer, and you have a gun with only two bullets, what do you do?
A: Shoot the lawyer twice.

Q: What do you get when you cross the Godfather with a lawyer?
A: An offer you can't understand.

Q: What is a criminal lawyer?
A: Redundant.

Q: What's the difference between a good lawyer and a great lawyer?
A: A good lawyer knows the law. A great lawyer knows the judge.

In the forty-plus years I've practiced law, I can honestly say I've met more "asshole attorneys" and "fuckin' lawyers" than I can count. Some are now my ex-partners. All too many lawyers have egos well beyond their intellect. For all I know, I'm one of them. Many lawyers are consistently blind to what's best for their clients. They just want to win and show they've got bigger balls than the other guy and whatever the equivalent would be for women lawyers. The problem is gender neutral.

When I ran a law firm, we remodeled our space. After I assigned offices, one of the male partners stormed into my office and demanded to know why a woman partner was given an office six inches wider than his.

"How could you possibly know the difference?" I asked. "Did you actually measure it?"

"No, I counted the ceiling tiles and she has one half a tile more than me. That's six inches."

While my first inclination was to throw him out of my office, I couldn't resist.

"Really? What won't you do for another six inches?"

He didn't laugh. I thought it was hilarious.

Don't get me wrong. I've known some great lawyers. Most of the lawyers I know are men and women who are incredibly smart and who care about their clients and colleagues. Today, I'm lucky and have not had to work with any "asshole attorneys" or "fuckin' lawyers" in my firm. We've had some. But they eventually quit and went to other firms, where colleagues of similar shark mentality reside.

In the first week I was with Reed Smith, I wrote an email to all the partners asking a question about a case. It was a short single-sentence message. No niceties. Just the question.

In minutes, I got multiple responses. But it was not the answers that struck me. At least three of the messages I received began: "Doug, welcome to the firm. In emails like this, we usually start out with 'Pardon the interruption.'" What a polite way to tell me, "Hey, you jerk New Yorker, have some cordiality when you interrupt someone else's day." It was refreshing.

I called one of my partners in Pittsburgh, the firm's headquarters, and told her how much I liked her response and how pleased I was to see that a Midwestern ethic existed at the firm, making working there all the more pleasant.

She politely responded, "You're such a New Yorker! Pittsburgh is not in the Midwest. We're in the same time zone as you are."

I couldn't help thinking, as an asshole New Yorker, Sorry, everything west of the Delaware River and east of California is the Midwest, that vast wasteland between New York and Los Angeles. I refrained and instead chose to laugh.

And for all I know, there are lawyers who think I'm an asshole attorney. And they may be right. But considering those whom I suspect felt that way, I consider it a compliment.

So keep it coming. Kick lawyers when we're up or when we're down. We've earned it.

chapter 31
The Party of We

How often do we hear today about how divided our nation is? If you believe the prognosticators, we're doomed and our society is crumbling. And gauging our nation's—and the world's—future peace and prosperity from the rhetoric we hear in Washington, Moscow, Pyongyang, Beijing, and Damascus, what we watch on Fox, CNN and MSNBC, and we read in the *Drudge Report*, *Breitbart*, and the *New York Times*, there is no hope.

Call me naive, but I don't buy it.

We don't have a divided nation. What we have is a collection of dismal leaders in Washington and in state capitals who don't know how to govern any more than a one-year-old knows how to explain Einstein's theory of relativity. Couple that with a collection of media that has lost its ethics and moved to private agendas rather than simply reporting facts as good journalists, something that was once considered a worthy profession.

But is the division really that deep?

It's not like this is the first time our nation has been in bitter dispute. There were more than a few colonists in 1776 who would have preferred the King to Congress. And many of them no doubt welcomed the invasion by the British in 1812. What about debates over the Trail of Tears, when we forced Native Americans from their homelands in 1831? Could we really be more divided today than we were in 1861 as we began the Civil

War? And no doubt the isolationists divided us in World War I. We suffered with great division in the Depression. In World War II, we interned innocent Japanese and denied them the due process allegedly guaranteed by the Constitution. We all witnessed the division in our nation when Americans spit on veterans when they returned from the Vietnam War. And that's just a partial list of moments in our history when we were divided.

Yet we not only worked through those tough times, we prospered when great leadership fueled by the people of our nation brought us together. How they did it was not about which party they came from. History shows us that neither the Democratic nor Republican parties have been consistent in their positions throughout history. Any member of a party who denies this is a total hypocrite.

It was with this background that in 2011 I launched the Party of We (www.PartyofWe.org). Its mission was to encourage and support free and responsible expression throughout the online and mobile ecosystems.

At the time—before Donald Trump tweeted about covfefe, Hillary Clinton erased 33,000 emails, Chuck Schumer fell in love with any camera pointed in his direction, or John Boehner was holding back his tears—the Internet had become our center of conversation. Actually, speaking to one another fell prey to SMS, email, and Facebook. Suddenly, carpal tunnel syndrome became a national malady suffered by millions of people glued to the keyboards of their computers.

When I launched Party of We, I made the following observation:

Everyone and anyone who uses the internet or any mobile digital platform for conversations or commerce is a member of the Party of We—a global collective—free from labels dictated by terrestrial borders, ideologies, or politics. When mobilized and united for a cause or principle, the Party of We can change the world, by toppling governments and influencing international policies or by simply making a product into a global success. The Party of We acknowledges no terrestrial borders except when in support of its mission. The power of the Party of We is pure and cannot be suppressed. It can be used for both good and evil, although the distinction can differ substantially depending upon issues and perspectives. Keep in mind that, virtually by definition, there is never unanimity in the Party of We. Most of all, at the end of the day, no individual or government can stop the Power of the We

I thought it was pretty cool, and convinced I'd get millions of subscribers. Then I'd be able to sell advertising space and retire. Look out, Mark Zuckerberg, I'm coming after you. And unlike you, Mr. Zuckerberg, no one will accuse me of stealing the idea.

The website is beautiful. Interactive. Allows posts by anyone. Includes a way to vote favorably or unfavorably on opinions expressed on the site, not just "likes." A guaranteed winner, right?

Wrong.

For reasons others can offer, the Party of We started off well and then quickly faded. While some of the posts were prophetic and harbingers of the future, that didn't seem to matter. Today, it's simply a repository of old articles and nothing has been posted in years. God only knows why I keep paying to have it live on the Internet. Most likely my ego.

But one article in particular got a good number of comments, good and bad. It's as pertinent today as it was on September 19, 2012, when I wrote:

> What Informs Us, Separates Us
>
> On the September 18th NBC *Today Show*, Matt Lauer interviewed Dick Costolo, CEO of Twitter, about what was hyped as a big announcement on changes to the texting service. In truth, the changes, all visual in nature, were a big yawn, but that wasn't what impressed me about the segment. Lauer asked Costolo, referring to Costolo's statement two years earlier that his goal was to find a "purpose" for Twitter long term, whether he had found that purpose. Costolo responded, "Twitter brings you closer." I guess that's now its long-term purpose. Bring us closer together.
>
> Unfortunately, Mr. Costolo couldn't be further from the truth. If Twitter has done anything, it has driven us apart. So has Facebook, LinkedIn, and just about every other social media application on the internet and mobile media.
>
> Sure, reports claim Twitter empowered people in the Arab Spring. And it has done more for free speech in just a few years than has 200-plus years of American jurisprudence. Twitter has led the way in bringing us information in a millisecond where we

used to wait for hours or even days. Yes, this year Twitter will be a vital source for the ins and outs, the truths and lies of the US presidential election. No wonder in four short years its value has rocketed to over $8 billion! But one would be a fool if they thought Twitter or any social media platform is bringing the world together after witnessing how it has contributed to the current violence over the film on the Prophet Muhammad and the photos posted and divisiveness reported at any number of sites. As I wrote in one of the first blogs on Party of We (and many others have said), the internet, for all of the great things it has brought us, has a very dark side as well.

But Twitter—and social media in general—does not and never will, bring anyone, anywhere closer together. Quite the opposite. People like Mr. Costolo have to stop drinking Mark Zuckerberg's Kool-Aid.

If readers would like a chilling explanation why, I strongly urge them to read Andrew Keen's new book, *Digital Vertigo—How Today's Online Social Revolution is Dividing, Diminishing and Disorienting Us.* In his book, Keen traces the evolution of social discourse from Aristotle to Mark Zuckerberg and tells a compelling story of how our increasing reliance on impersonal, largely anonymous, texting and posting has torn apart families, friends, and the basic fabric of society.

In a nutshell, we barely talk to one another anymore. We no longer have discussions that include any meaningful or thought-provoking dialog. Increasingly, all our communications—and what we do as a result of them—are via a process of short messages or posts on services like Twitter and Facebook. We look down more than we look up. Our thumbs move more than our lips. We touch keyboards more than we touch one another. And God forbid that we should ever pick up a ball point pen and actually write someone a letter by hand.

I'm not saying no one talks or communicates in person anymore. Sure we do. But less than we used to. A lot less.

Do you now text your friends, colleagues, siblings, parents, and children more often than you call them on the phone? It was three years ago that texting outpaced voice on cell phones. Think about that for a moment. Voices on telephones took a backseat to typing!

How often do you email your co-worker down the hall with a question rather than get up and take a walk to actually look at them in the eye? How often do you call a restaurant for a reservation anymore? In the last couple of years, have your buying habits shifted from strolling in a retail mall to clicking through an online e-tailer? I could go on and on with the list. The point is simple—social media and technology is replacing personal interaction between you and me and everyone else. Maybe some of it is simple and trite, but I wonder if anyone thought that what started as a curious SMS service with a limit of 140 characters would today become more than 200 million tweets every day. No one could have anticipated that, and no one can anticipate the extent of damage social media will exact on social discourse as the digital future unfolds.

In a way, this grand evolution of technology reminds me of a line in the wonderful Alan Jackson song, "I'll Go On Loving You": "I don't know what brought us together. What strange forces of nature conspire to construct the present from the past." Except this time, those forces of nature are bits and bytes that are conspiring to construct our future from the present and destroy the past.

Last year, in an editorial in the *New York Times*, Sherry Turkle, professor at MIT, psychologist, and author of *Alone Together: Why We Expect More from Technology and Less from Each Other*, wrote:

"I spend the summers at a cottage on Cape Cod, and for decades I walked the same dunes that Thoreau once walked. Not too long ago, people walked with their heads up, looking at the water, the sky, the sand and at one another, talking. Now they often walk with their heads down, typing. Even when they are with friends, partners, children, everyone is on their own devices. So I say, look up, look at one another, and let's start the conversation."

Alas, Dr. Turkle, I think it's too late. But maybe someone out there will come up with the true killer app. One that kills texting for a while. Shuts down posting. Puts Twitter, Facebook, LinkedIn and all their brethren on holiday once in a while. One that lets phones only be phones and thumbs just part of a handshake. An app that forces you to buy your next shirt or blouse from a living store clerk, not an avatar. We need it before what we do less and less of today becomes nothing more than a memory in history, like horse-drawn carriages and gas lamps. Now that would be worth downloading!

Don't get me wrong. I'm all for progress and the wonders technology and the internet have given us. I just wish we'd find a way—a discipline—that could preserve our personal interaction in a global community that has so much to offer beyond 140 characters.

The post received some interesting responses. This one came in from *social-allie*:

This story is unfortunately an uninformed and one-sided assessment of the capabilities of social networks. This author clearly doesn't have his finger on the pulse of social media and hasn't done enough research before forming and communicating his opinion.

People can use any medium to create hate and foster mean energies.

But social media has enabled communities to help rebuild and connect after disasters.

Twitter, and other social networks, have created lasting friendships.

And Twitter has the ability to keep the population more informed than any other medium.

If that's not bringing people together . . . then I don't know what is.

BHB101 wrote:

The consequences of our younger population spending so much time glued to electronic gadgets, while spurning a more traditional, face-to-face interactive education might, at first, seem like a good way to merge universal knowledge and blend the thoughts of the masses together . . . and, in a perfect world, that might build a more homogeneous, peaceful planet.

Unfortunately, the truth is that it is much more likely to be a destructive and divisive force, building an invisible obstacle to personal and intellectual growth with others, and eschewing the historical benefit of cultural assimilation, which is probably needed in today's America more than ever before.

In the same way that some progressive school curriculum administrators want to develop avant-garde programs, and introduce cutting edge, diverse stories and books for our children to read, the overwhelming cohesive good of studying the traditional classics (albeit in different ways, and from different teachers' points of view) is one way that we have historically been able to bind a diverse population into a country where the same values and traditions are the very essence of how "foreigners" become one of the "us" and "we" become culturally bound together by the inclusion of new points of view.

Being caught in a sterile bubble of electronic communications, without the sunlight of outside discussions, personal interactions, and traditional studies that serve to assimilate outsiders, the effect makes everyone an outsider, as opposed to becoming more tolerant and homogeneous as a nation.

I suspect that the recent announcement that the latest national SAT scores are the lowest in 40 years says something about the lack of knowledge, writing ability, and intellectual capabilities that we are letting pass for education, and that, perhaps, we are not demanding enough face-time from our children.

To which *mwbecker* replied:

social_allie, I'm afraid you may be drinking the same Kool-Aid as Mr. Costolo. Mr. Wood is not saying that social media and the internet have not done wonderful things for communications between people and empowering ideas. social allie, you should read his other articles on the site. More importantly, the links provided to Keen and Turkle also prove the point of empowerment and information, but more so support Wood's view that social media, as a whole, does not bring people together—as individuals who can really truly touch and be touched. Read Keen's book. There is more authority in his treatise than all the links to love stories on Facebook combined. Anecdote does not prove reality. Scholarship like Keen's does. Read it. Like becker.randolph said, "Social media, the internet, e-mailing are all great tools, but they can never replace the free flowing of ideas that occur when one is sharing one-on-one time together with another, in person." And that's the worst of what Twitter and other social media platforms do. I have no problem with their sales pitches. But tell the truth. Don't ask me to drink your Kool-Aid. It is socially irresponsible for companies like Twitter to tell only one side of the story—the good and not the overwhelming bad. I'm not saying the benefits are not worth the pain, but let's all be honest. Or as Professor Turkle put it, "So I say, look up, look at one another, and let's start the conversation."

I responded to *social-allie*:

To social_allie—Thank you for commenting on my post. Your observations are good ones, but I have never said the internet does not do positive things. Quite to the contrary. But I continue to believe that while it may occasionally bring people together, e.g., some of the examples you cite, on the whole it has clearly done the exact opposite. I think the scholarly writings of people like Keen, Turkle and others a lot smarter than I am bear that out.

As someone who counsels companies and individuals every day on how to legally use the internet, it never ceases to amaze me how it has been such a yin and a yang for society. I've covered all the good things many times on this website. Please indulge me for a few more observations on what the internet has done to harm the individual in every one of us:

1. It has fed us with an insatiable need for speed. We can't get enough bytes per second. Even when we don't need them. We keep upgrading and spending money for faster rates that

we barely notice. In turn, that appetite causes us to:

2. Lose our patience. Everything has to happen now. We refuse to wait. People must respond immediately or we feel offended, left out. If we hear our mobile devices beep or our email notice pop up, we rush to reply lest we cause the person on the other end of the messaging to lose their patience. In turn, this causes us to:

3. Lose our civility. We react too quickly. Too emotionally. We email, post, and tweet without thinking first. Who will see it? Who might it offend? Who can it hurt? No one can deny that today some of the most awful and offensive things one can imagine are routinely posted on the internet by people who would never think of displaying such trash on the wall of their homes or take an ad out in the *New York Times* to say it or show it. The internet has simply made too many people downright nasty. A lot nastier than we've ever been. That's a sad reality.

In the end, the internet is perhaps the most wonderful advance in our lifetimes. Over time, this Information Revolution we're experiencing will be seen as a transformative time for mankind. And we cannot turn back the clock to a more nostalgic time. But we should never forget the days when we used to stop by to say hello, write a thank you note on paper and mail it, or simply phone a friend just to talk. There is no question the internet is making such past behavior rarer day by day. If we do forget that, the interaction we all miss will become the relic of history I fear and that, social_allie, would be a true tragedy.

Later, *scottydubs* wrote:

> What makes this discussion ironic to me is that we are debating the degree to which social media is bringing us together via a social media forum—blogging. While I see both sides to the argument, I can't help but notice that we are having a non-face-to-face yet highly intellectual discussion. I have no clue who any of you are: *becker.randolph, social_allie, mwbecker or BHB 101*. When would we collectively get together and have this discussion over a delicious coffee or an alcoholic beverage? Highly unlikely! Sure this might not be bringing us closer together physically, but virtually, I am enjoying our interaction. The effort required to articulate my thoughts and choose my words wisely is intellectually stimulating. With my friends, I would surely rather discuss mindless topics face-to-face such as sports, TV shows and where we should eat dinner. But then again, I am sure I have pissed off a lot of people who might have been trying to have a conversation with me as I read and respond to this blog.

So where are we today and what does this have to do with a supposedly divided nation?

I suggest we are no worse off nor better off with the president's tweets, Clinton's lost emails, Chuck Schumer's infatuation with cameras, or John Boehner's tears today than we were then or any other time in our history. As much as social_allie, mwbecker, scottydubs, or I may debate whether the internet brings us together or not, no one can realistically debate that politicians and media are not bringing us together. Indeed, the dialog among the four of us in the brief discourse we had on Party of We puts the Internet—and being united—in perspective far better than any of the talking heads in Washington, Moscow, Pyongyang, Beijing, and Damascus, on Fox, CNN and MSNBC, or in the *Drudge Report*, *Breitbart*, and the *New York Times* combined.

When will they listen?

More important, when will someone offer me millions for PartyofWe.org? It's for sale.

chapter 32
Parting Shots

Change is not a bad thing, no matter how much it hurts your ego when it first occurs. That's not to say you shouldn't be angry and hurt, but the adage is absolutely true that time heals all wounds. The healing may be slow, but the healing happens.

Whether that's true is a little more challenging. So far, my ego has survived all of the attacks.

Don't mistake fear of your leadership as loyalty or respect. There's nothing more enlightening than to see how fast people jump ship who you would have thought would stand with you. I saw it at Hall Dickler.

Learn to understand that being abandoned by those who you feel you led well for years is not a reflection on you. It's a reflection on them. That's why they are led and you lead. Or so I'd like to think.

Watch closely how people treat others. Make no mistake. When they have the opportunity, they will treat you the same way. Don't be surprised. I only wish I could forget all the times this adage has proven to be true. Yet I am always surprised.

Do not expect loyalty from those you protect, nurture, or mentor. Their memory of what you did for them or meant to them fades quickly once they see greener pastures or believe they can do better. But when they leave, hold no grudge. Wish them well. And I suspect I should expect even less from those I've only known a short period of time, regardless of what I may have done for them. Memories are short.

Don't expect respect to be given for what you've done in the past when others want to make changes. In the end, each of us is expendable, no matter how optimistic we may try to be. But hopefully, however expendable we are, we can keep our dignity through the process.

Don't pre-judge who will be your allies when you need them. Many who do come to your side and support your views may sur- ́ prise you. You may have to change your judgment dramatically on those you would least expect to come to the plate and take a stand. I've often been pleasantly surprised when someone I assumed was on an opposite side of an argument agrees with me. In hindsight, I usually see that I had no reason to be surprised. Truthfully, the person was there all along. I just didn't see it.

Don't lose faith in yourself. Remember that something got you to your position of leadership, particularly if that leadership lasted for a significant period of time. Fall back on those strengths and rebuild from there. That has been my saving grace.

Learn to let go and remember that the material things are not really that important. Integrity counts most. Don't lose that ideal. Perhaps true, but that Ferrari sure looks good.

"Forgive and forget" works for priests and nuns. Don't worry about trying to find a way to forgive. If forgiving is not comfortable for you, then don't do it. It will waste too much of your time. But do learn to forget. Forget the anger, the feeling for revenge, and the need to win. This one I really take to heart and find a way to move on with my emotions.

Being removed from power, however unceremonious or disrespectful that removal may be, is not a reflection on you, but on those who made the change. Short of fraud or criminal behavior on your part, they are the wrongdoers, not you. This one's tough to believe when you feel like the loser. But over time, it's always true.

Don't make rash decisions. Quick emotional decisions are more likely to hurt you than help you. Be patient. Chances are those who now have the control they coveted will learn for themselves how difficult it is to lead. More likely than not, they'll fail. Right. Easier said than done.

Voice your views, but do so logically and calmly, avoiding as much emotion as you can muster. When the emotion comes through, don't lament too long over it. Move on. Over the past forty years, I've done my fair share of moving on and don't regret it.

Follow the twenty-four-hour rule. Let any decision you feel you must make sit for twenty-four hours. Then write out the decision you must make, including the pros and cons of doing so. Be smart, not hasty. Too bad I'm Irish. This rule never works for me.

acknowledgments

Many people made this book possible. Without them, I would have never been able to complete it. Thanks go to Nancy Schulein, my assistant of more than 20 years, for making sure my memories of events she witnessed were accurate, and to my personal attorney, Anthony Davis, for his advice and counsel on the book and throughout my years practicing. Thanks also go to the team my publisher, Plum Bay Publishing, put together to review and edit my writing and layout of the manuscript — Jeremy N. Townsend, Kate Petrella, and Barbara Aronica-Buck. A very special thanks goes to Lauren Harvey for the wonderful cover design. I've known Lauren since she was born and have proudly watched her grow into an amazing artist. And thank you to my friend Mitch Becker for reading early drafts and providing critical commentary. Last and certainly not least, I owe great thanks to my publicists, Claire McKinney and Larissa Ackerman, for their counseling and advice on how to make my writing resonate with readers.

JUL 1 0 2018

9 780998 861722